THE PRACTICAL MARKETING HANDBOOK OF DEFINITIONS

Second Edition

Researched and Edited

By

Michael C. Walker

authorHOUSE

1663 LIBERTY DRIVE, SUITE 200
BLOOMINGTON, INDIANA 47403
(800) 839-8640
www.authorhouse.com

First published by AuthorHouse 07/29/04

ISBN: 1-4184-5690-X (e-book)
ISBN: 1-4184-3693-3 (Paperback)

Library of Congress Control Number: 2003097689

This book is printed on acid free paper.

Printed in the United States of America
Bloomington, IN

This book is dedicated to marketing students of all ages.

Other Books By The Author

- An Introduction to Bank Marketing Research

- Marketing to Seniors

- Home Delivered Services:
  Building and Maintaining Your Program

Preface

Flash back to 1969. In the past thirty-plus years, there have been many developments and improvements in business in general and marketing in particular. Principles have remained relatively constant, but the conduct of marketing disciplines has continued to grow both in complexity and efficiency. Personal computers, the internet and e-mail did not exist in 1969. Nor did cable television, fax machines or cell phones, and television was black and white. Credit card networks, such as Visa and Master Card, were only in their infancy, covering a very small part of the United States and even less internationally. Desk top photo copiers were still in the trial stage and were neither very good nor dependable. Consequently, carbon copy paper was still an essential staple in office supplies.

While a graduate student at the time, I had many opportunities to use marketing reference sources, however few consistently met my needs. There were glossaries, dictionaries, encyclopedias and other resources available, but the material was often lacking in substance or plain English. Some sources were incomplete and others cumbersome to use.

As a research project, I decided to compile an easy to use marketing resource of my own. A wide variety of sources were researched and select marketing definitions were edited with the potential reader in mind.

The final edited product was deemed good enough to be published as *The Practical Marketing Handbook of Definitions.* This was a limited edition produced solely for libraries. That was 1969, and I am proud to say that copies are still carried on some library shelves.

Now, fast forward to 2004. *The Practical Marketing Handbook of Definitions* was overdue for updating and expanded availability. This second edition has been designed to be even more useable while in a compact format. It contains more marketing and related definitions than the first edition, but with less statistical terminology. The research and editing has been completely updated and re-edited, and definitions expanded to broaden usefulness. This edition is designed to be a most useful resource for the professional and the student alike.

Rochester, New York
March, 2004

A

A.B.C.
Audit Bureau of Circulation is a non-profit publishers' audit service for reporting circulation figures on subscription and newsstand sales at required intervals. Headquarters: 900 N. Meacham Road, Schaumburg, IL 60173-4968.

A.M.A.
American Management Association. A non-profit membership based organization providing a full range of management development and educational services. Located: 1601 Broadway, New York, New York 10019.

A.M.A.
American Marketing Association. A non-profit educational service association of marketing professionals and students in marketing. Headquarters: 311 South Wacker Drive, Suite 5800, Chicago, IL 60606.

Account Aging
A credit control method of reporting account balances by the number of days balances are past due. Typical periods used are current, 30 days, 60 days, 90 days and 120 days and over. Important for future sales consideration to delinquent

accounts. Some organizations require support from sales personnel in the the collection of past due accounts.

Account Openers
Premiums or freebies given as incentives to open an account at a bank, department store or other goods and services providers. These types of incentives are used to build traffic for new relationships or new branch locations.

Account Representative
One who represents the organization in a given market may be assigned specific new business goals over a given time period. Typically the responsibility is for making sales and establishing new relations.

Account Retention
A measurement of the time accounts remain open and active for any given period, and the ability to retain customers measured against a specific goal. There may be noticeable differences in open vs. active accounts, and decisions need to be made on what to do with open, but inactive accounts. How long should inactive accounts be kept open and how to get them active are important marketing questions.

Accounts Receivable

Term generally applied to unpaid credit balances owed. Such balances are typically lumped together by select time periods for an overall assessment of the condition of receivables. Common reporting periods are 30, 60, 90 and 120 days and over.

Acronym

A created "word" using the first letter of several words as a form of abbreviated title. Such creations are often used for promotional purposes, and sometimes become trade or brand names.

Action Item

Part of an action plan or other agenda needing prescribed attention, generally with an assignment of responsibility within a given timeframe.

Action Plan

A means by which to reach a particular goal. Typically an objective, e.g., in a strategic plan, contains one or more goals which in turn may contain one or more action plans.

Active Account

An open account, sometimes with a current balance owed, where there has been some transaction of business over a given period, e.g., three to six months.

Activity Report

A report of sales volume over a given period that may be broken down by salesperson, area or time period, and consolidated for meaningful comparison to previous and future reports.

Adequate Sample

A survey sample containing a sufficient number of potential respondents representative of the total universe from which the sample was taken. This is measured by formula or by a table of confidence levels per sample size and universe.

Adoption Process

The process that a person goes through in accepting a new product or service introduced to the market. The process moves from innovation through actual adoption or use of the product or service.

Advanced Premium

An immediate offer of a premium incentive to a customer who is willing to make a firm commitment for a future purchase. Sometimes used as an introduction to new products, services or programs where the new item is not "take-home ready."

Advertiser's Index
A list of publication advertisers alphabetically by name, typically found at the back of business, trade and other magazines.

Advertising Allowance
Monies provided by a manufacturer or supplier to the seller for advertising their products or services. Typically based upon prior business volumes. This may be done as part of a cooperative promotional venture.

Advertising Campaign
A coordinated program of advertising with a principal theme and goal, usually run for a specific time period, and often part of a more comprehensive marketing campaign.

Advertising Effectiveness Analysis
A study designed to determine the degree to which an advertisement, a campaign or promotion has accomplished pre-designed objectives. Requires survey research of the targeted audience.

Advertising Flyer or Flier
A promotional message conveyed by insertion in magazines and newspapers or distributed as handouts. "Take one" racks are another means of distribution.

Advertising Premiums
See Advertising Specialties.

Advertising Psychology
The employment of psychology principles to promotional practices. This typically involves the use of behavioral science and psychographics in advertising strategy.

Advertising Reserve
A contingency fund set aside for advertising needs beyond the scope of a budgeted and planned period of time. Used to offset of unanticipated competitive pressures.

Advertising Rhythm
A quality or style of an advertisement to guide the reader, listener or viewer through the message in a systematic flowing manner. Usually developed through a variety of pre-testing to gauge audience reception and understanding.

Advertising Specialties
Premiums or nominal gifts given out as a means of advertising. Items such as pens, key rings and memo pads bearing an advertising message are typical examples.

Advertising Style
The general appearance and basic emphasis of an advertisement or series of advertisements. May include the use of words and pictures in a given format. This can be an important feature for frequent advertisers in an effort to keep in touch with their customers.

Advertising Tie-in
A cooperative advertisement or promotion with a national or regional product or service provider. This can provide cost and credibility benefits to the local seller or provider, enhancing exposure.

Affinity Marketing
The promotion of goods and services to certain groups or clubs because of the make up of the memberships, and generally at preferred rates and terms.

Affordable Advertising Method
A basis used to prepare advertising budgets where amounts are determined largely on what the organization can afford. To be effective, this approach must be balanced with the advertiser's anticipated needs.

Agate Line
A standard unit of measure for advertisement size in a publication. Newspaper advertising rates are typically measured per agate line.

Aged
Another term formerly used to refer to seniors, but now occasionally used to reference those in the upper levels of the age spectrum. Today, members of this market are referred to as seniors. Those 85 years of age and older are sometimes referred to as elderly or aged.

Agency Contract
A contractual agreement between an advertising agency and the client including specific terms and conditions. The contract will likely specify that this agency will coordinate all of the organization's advertising needs.

Agency of Record
An organization's designated agency through which all media advertising placements are made on a fee basis. Sometimes set up on a base retainer plus fees schedule.

Agent
One who is authorized by contract to act on behalf of a client in select business matters for a fee or

commission. This may be either an individual or an organization.

AIDA Theory

A selling concept identifying four stages that a buyer mentally passes through before making a purchase. These are Attention, Interest, Desire and Action. The theory holds that this is a progressive process that is not likely to advance to successive stages without first getting the buyer's attention.

Aided Recall

Used in personal survey research interviewing, the respondent is given set clues in order to direct their response to a given question or subject, but not coached to a desired response.

Allowance

An incentive provided by manufacturers and distributors to retailers in return for promotional or display consideration.

Alphabetic Sampling

A survey sampling technique used by researchers to develop a representative sample from a universe of large or unknown dimension, using an alphabetical selection process.

Altruistic Advertising
Promotion for charitable causes or campaigns with an appeal to the satisfaction of having given at a time and choice of need.

Appeal
A distinct characteristic of a product or service that draws customer interest by an affinity to basic instincts. This becomes an important marketing challenge.

Applause Mail
Written responses, solicited or unsolicited, sent in by readers, listeners or viewers in reaction to a message or presentation. Important information for the design of products, services or marketing campaigns.

Approach
The first step in a sales call where the goal is to introduce the parties, and to gain the attention of the prospective buyer.

Area Sampling
A technique used where a larger geographical area is divided up into a number of sub-areas for sampling purposes to provide a more representative sample. Typically a sample percentage will be applied to each sub-area in an effort to

obtain proportionate representation. See Cluster Sampling.

Arithmetic Mean

An average obtained by totaling the sum values of observations and dividing by the total number of those observations.

Association Test

A research technique designed to measure a respondent's association with particular products and services. It is important to know if respondents can associate products or services with the correct provider.

Attention Getter

An advertising term used to describe the focus of attention in an advertisement. Used to draw in the reader, viewer or listener in an effort to get them to stay with that message.

Attention Value

The ability of a promotion or product to attract prospective customer attention because of special qualities such as color, size, packaging or means of display. This requires a marketing research application to measure the attention value by quality by degree.

Attitude
The characteristics a person shows toward a particular thing or concept, including degrees of feelings and opinions. A psychographic characteristic.

Attitudinal Research
Consumer research directed to the study of attitudes toward particular brands, products, services, programs and organizations. Important in designing advertising strategy.

Attrition
The loss of customers due to a variety of variables including state of health, death, dissatisfaction, lack of need, re-location and competitive factors. Sales forecasts cannot be accurately produced without measuring attrition loss. See Turnover.

Audience Awareness
The relative knowledge of a product, service or promotion by a select group of respondents, as measured by marketing research.

Audience Grid
A graphic presentation to measure product or service acceptability by various audience types, produced as a result of marketing research.

Audience Measure

Research designed to measure the size and specific characteristics of a designated audience to a communication medium or message. May be accomplished through home audience response systems, telephone interviews or various other research formats.

Audience Share

A percentage of the total audience universe reached by a promotional communication or broadcast program, typically measured by direct response or survey sample.

Augmented Cash Guarantee

A commitment by the manufacturer, distributor or provider of a product or service to refund the customer more than the purchase price, if not fully satisfied. For example, refunding 110% of the purchase price under specific conditions.

Augmented Product/Service

Services and other benefits produced and sold as enhancements to a product or service. These can provide support to the customer and additional revenue to the provider.

Authorized Dealer

An organization that has a contractual relationship with a manufacturer. Many such arrangements are confined to specific products or geographical areas, such as an exclusive relationship.

Awareness

The first step in the process of learning about a new product or service, where the prospective customer begins a process of internalizing the potential benefits and transforms this to interest. See AIDA Theory.

B

Baby Boomer
A contemporary term used to describe a sizeable consumer group made up of those born between the end of World War II and the mid 1960's. They represent an attractive marketing target due both to the group's size and purchasing power. This group will shape the senior market of the future.

Back Cover
The outside back cover of a magazine or similar publication, sometimes called the fourth cover. This is considered a prime advertising location.

Back Order
An order for merchandise that is temporarily out of stock, and an order to be filled upon replenishment of stock is filed.

Bad Debt Allowance
A reserve for potential delinquent account charge offs based upon historical experience or best estimate forecasts.

Bailment
A contractual arrangement whereby goods are delivered to an agent to be held for a specific

purpose and time period, within specified liability limits.

Bait and Switch
An unethical and sometimes illegal practice where an advertised "bait" is used to bring in customers. The customers are then pressured to buy similar, but more expensive items. The salesperson is also under pressure to "sell up" from the bait advertised.

Balance
The relative composition of an advertisement where the proportions of copy and picture are sufficient to create a balance to meet the message goal.

Balloon Copy
Advertising messages containing cartoon caricatures with their words in balloon captions. Typically used to portray a specific situation promoting a product, service or other message.

Ballpark Estimate
An approximation provided for the sake of discussion where exact figures or known estimates are not available.

Banner
A display message printed on a synthetic material, cloth hanging or a flag hung by rope cord or chain.

Often used to announce grand openings, special sales or serve as temporary signage.

Barter

The exchange of goods or services in lieu of payment. In marketing, a barter trade may provide an opportunity to obtain advertising coverage in exchange for goods or services. Income realized from a barter is generally taxable.

Base Rate

An amount charged by an advertising medium for an advertisement prior to any application of discounts, credits or other offsets.

Bayes' Theorem

Named for Reverend Thomas Bayes, an amateur mathematician, the Theorem provides a statistical approach to making decisions based on probabilities under known conditions. Used to construct statistical models to aid in marketing decision making. In simplest form, constructing a tree diagram provides for schematic observation.

Behavioral Sciences

An inclusive term covering the application of theories and practices from the fields of psychology, sociology, social psychology and cultural anthropology to the study of consumer motivations and behavioral patterns.

Believability

A consideration in preparing advertising and promotional messages as to the extent to which there may be consumer acceptance or a willingness to identify with a product, service or program. This may be pre-tested by means of marketing research to increase the probability of success.

Benchmark

An acceptable chosen standard by which to measure performance by an organization or program. Typically the best practices are chosen for a target challenge.

Bias

In conjunction with marketing research, a prejudice interjected into a survey by interviewer judgment or by improper sampling techniques, producing questionable results.

Bid

An offer to purchase or provide goods or services at a specific price. Bids are often solicited by invitation, and some organizations must use a bid process for purchases over a certain dollar amount.

Big Ticket

Term used to qualify certain products or services as more expensive ones with bigger price tags.

Bill Insert

A promotional or informational piece placed in the mailing envelope along with the monthly statement. Sometimes called a statement stuffer or simply an insert.

Bill Stuffer

See Bill Insert.

Bleed

Where printed material or advertising copy uses all space to the full extent of the page, with no white or plain margins, in a magazine, newspaper or similar publication.

Blind Advertisements

Advertisements that do not include the advertiser's name or address. Often used in employment ads, both in display and classified form.

Blind Headlines

A commonly used term in advertising where there is no lead-in statement offering a clue to the message content. The intent is to entice the reader to read the full message.

Blind Offer

See Hidden Offer.

Blue Sky
Term used for looking into the future on an idea or concept with little or no historical perspective or experience. Depending on potential merit, may serve as the beginning of an idea for further investigation.

Blurb
A brief description of a product, service or program used in short advertising or publicity releases.

Boilerplate
Standard text in a promotional message or contractual agreement, based on time tested wording, used to explain legal points or limit liability.

Boldface Copy
Copy type in darker and sometimes larger print in advertising copy or other text material, such as contractual agreements, used for emphasis.

Border Line
The surrounding space or markings of an advertisement to set it off from other ads or copy.

Bottom Line
The net profit from business ventures, taking into account revenues and expenses. Also, used to

refer to the anticipated profit or loss projection for a marketing program.

Brainstorming

A collective process that promotes group discussion to come up with new ideas, suggestions and problem solutions.

Brand

A name, symbol, or other designation used to identify particular goods or services of a provider to differentiate them from those of other providers. Brand names are valuable exclusive property typically protected by registered trademarks or service marks.

Brand Association

The degree to which there is consumer association of a brand with a particular product or service in a given product or service category.

Brand Awareness

Market knowledge of a specific product, service or company by virtue of a brand name. This is an important factor in the recognition and acceptance to promotional and purchase offers.

Brand Buyers
A label given to consumers who make purchases by brand name rather than price, quality or other factors.

Brand Conscious
The relative consumer knowledge of particular brands of products or services, and the tendency to repeat purchase them.

Brand Loyalty
The degree to which there is consumer attachment, through continued use, to particular lines of products or services. This is an extension of brand consciousness.

Brand Preference
A selective preference for particular brands of products or services over other competing brands, based on firsthand knowledge or strong recommendation and promotional reinforcement.

Brand Rating
The measurement of consumer preference to particular brands of products or services against competing brands in the market through survey research.

Brand Switching

A change in consumer preference for specific brands of products or services by the influence of others, promotional impact or dissatisfaction based on use.

Break-Even Analysis

A financial study to determine the relationship between total revenue and total cost for a product, service or program at varying price levels.

Break-Even Point

A statistical measurement to demonstrate the point at which sufficient sales revenue will cover fixed and variable costs for a product, service or program.

Broadside

A large paper or cardboard printed on one side to be used as a poster for advertising and promotional purposes, typically affixed to the outside of a building or internal wall.

Bulk Mail

Catalogs, circulars and other similar pieces sorted by zip code and mailed together at a special bulk mail rate.

Bumper Banner
An advertising or promotional message attached to the bumper of a road vehicle. A form of bumper sticker used for promotional purposes.

Buried Offer
See Hidden Offer.

Business Exchange Clubs
Groups of business representatives and independent contractors whose members meet on a regular schedule to exchange business leads and new contacts. This represents an organized networking opportunity.

Business Reply Mail
Mail that is pre-stamped and pre-addressed for convenient return by the recipient. Mailing documents prepared for return may be envelopes, post cards, labels or containers.

Buyer
The customer or purchaser of a product or service to whom the marketing approach is directed. However, it must be recognized that the buyer may not always be the user of the purchased object. This is particularly important in purchases for kids and the elderly.

Buyer Learning Curve
A statistical or graphical presentation designed to measure market awareness or acceptance of particular products, services or programs over time.

Buyer Readiness
The degree to which a purchaser is prepared to act. This will include awareness, knowledge, preference and commitment, for example.

Buyer's Market
A market condition where an abundance of goods exceeds consumer demand, allowing for below market purchasing opportunities.

Buying Agents
Individuals or organizations employed by buyers and buyer groups to research the market for the better deals on selected purchases, and making offers based on pre-defined levels of authority.

Buying Club
A formal group of customers buying merchandise at a lower cost because of increased purchasing power generated by the club's membership.

Buying Committee
A company group appointed to evaluate specified purchasing decisions based upon guidelines

provided for direction. Members typically are those who will be directly affected by the purchases chosen.

Buying Group
A formal group of organizations and institutions buying products and services collectively in larger quantities for greater discounts.

Buying Incentive
A provided reason for the customer to buy a specific product or service at a given time. Incentives may include reduced price, a coupon, a gift item, or trial offer.

Buying Power
The potential dollars available in a given market for the purchase of goods and services at a given point in time.

C

Call Back

A salesperson's return to a prospective buyer after an unsuccessful or incomplete first visit. Usually the approach will be adjusted to address initial objections, or respond to questions needing further support.

Call Card

A card left at the door or office after an unsuccessful attempt to make a sales contact. This may be a simple business card or a larger card containing more information, sometimes made to hang on a door knob or handle.

Call Report

A written report prepared by the salesperson upon the completion of a customer call. Whether the call was generated by the salesperson or the customer, specific information is captured in written form for future reference. This is especially important when the next contact is made by a different salesperson.

Call Write-up

See Call Report.

Callbacks

Survey respondents requiring a second call or visit because they were not available the first time. Beginning with design of the survey process, a decision should be made on how many attempts, or callbacks are to be given any potential respondent. This should then become a constant for that survey.

Campaign

A series of advertisements or promotional messages designed to run over a specified time period with a particular offer of a product, service or program. This may be part of a more comprehensive marketing effort including sales and publicity campaigns, for example.

Canned Program

A set program or message to be used over and over, without material deviation, typically used in sales for specific offers. Often called a canned presentation or selling formula, and also used in training newer salespeople.

Canvassing

Door to door or telephone contacts made from a list compiled for that purpose, but without previous prospect contact. Provides an opportunity for potential sales presentations and new business.

Captive Market
An area where there is virtually no competition for products or services of a particular organization. Generally considered to be a seller's market where terms and conditions can be dictated.

Car Card
Term used to describe an advertising sign or board on buses, subways and other forms of public transportation.

Caregiver
One who is taking care of a sick or infirmed person. May be a hired person or a member of the family, a neighbor or friend. Can be important in a marketing sense in that caregivers often make purchasing decisions and choices on behalf of those they care for.

Carrying Charge
An interest or service charge levied for buying products and services on time.

Cartoon Test
A projective technique using cartoons and other drawings for respondents to evaluate a message or theme. Often used to help design advertising copy. Cartoon drawings can be used to tell a story in a way to emphasize or de-emphasize various

aspects important to conveying a particular message.

Cash Allowance
A discount made available to retailers by wholesalers and distributors to encourage larger purchases. The larger the purchase, the greater the discount.

Cash and Carry
A marketing strategy typically used by smaller retailers to compete with larger or chain stores. It promotes lower prices in return for saving the cost of delivering and offering credit charges or collecting receivables.

Cash Cow
A substantial net revenue producer for an organization. It may represent a product, service or program that provides sufficient returns to help offset the expenses of other, less profitable operations.

Cash Discount
A discount on the purchase price of a product or service if payment is made in cash rather than by charge accounts or credit cards.

Cash Incentive

An inducement offered by the seller to customers who pay for their purchases up front at the time of order, rather than at the time of delivery.

Catalog House

A wholesaler who sells merchandise through catalogs by mail order. May sell to consumers as well as retailers. Some of these organizations open retail outlets as well.

Catch Phrase

An advertising term used to describe a one or few word statement designed to be remembered by the purchasing audience. These may include a coined phrase, jargon or an acronym, for example.

Cause Marketing

An initiative designed with a goal of mutual benefit, creating a partnership between commercial and not-for-profit organizations, to promote community based programs and other charitable causes.

Census Bureau

U.S. Census Bureau of the United States Department of Commerce, Washington, DC. Publisher of the National Data Book. Information available at: www.census.gov/statab/www/.

Census Tract
A geographical delineation by the United States Department of Commerce used for larger cities where they are broken down into approximately equal population centers with similar social and economic profiles.

Center Spread
The two middle pages of a magazine or other publication which open flat for continuous advertising opportunities.

Charge Account
An agreement between consumer and retailer for the payment of purchases over a specified time period. Terms such as time and finance charges are integral to the agreement.

Circular
A single page promotional piece that can be handed out, inserted in billing statements or magazines, mailed, or placed in a "take one" counter location.

Claim
In advertising a claim is a statement made about the product, service or organization highlighted in an advertisement, stressing a positive aspect or benefit to be realized through purchase and use.

Class Consciousness
An awareness of one's own social position relative to that of others on a specific or implied social scale.

Classified Advertising
Typically a section in a magazine, newspaper or similar publication where smaller worded or display advertisements are listed by category. The rates charged are often by the word and frequency of appearance, or by the space used within the column.

Client
An organization or individual who hires the services of another person, agent or firm. Services are usually of a professional nature such as legal, financial or advertising representative.

Close
The point in a sales presentation where there is an attempt to reach a meeting of the minds between salesperson and customer, and agree to purchase or not to purchase. It is important for the salesperson to know when to begin the closing process.

Closed-end Questions
Survey questions that provide specific choices for the respondent without allowing alternatives or interviewer interpretation. Provides for clear-cut

tabulation and evaluation, but without respondent qualification.

Closing
See Close.

Cluster Sampling
Process of dividing the population of a given area or other sampling units into many sub-groups and randomly selecting samples from these groups. Provides for a means to compare sub-groups as needed, but not possible in one larger population.

Clutter
The result of an overload of messages reaching a viewer or listener in a given time period. The goal for the advertiser is to get the message through the clutter, while the recipient needs to decide which, if any, of the messages to process.

Coaching
A part of the sales training process where the supervisor or a trainer guides the trainee through a variety of sales situations in an effort to support the complete training process.

Cognitive Dissonance
A theory of marketing psychology that describes consumer post-purchase dissatisfaction or negative feelings with or about the product or service

purchased. Provides an opportunity for the marketer to understand dissatisfaction and how it might be counteracted.

Coincidental Audience Testing

A method of measuring audience size and program acceptance by telephone interview or electronic data entry while the program is in progress. This is done on a sample basis for later projection.

Coined Phrase

One or more words originated by a provider of goods or services used to reference one or a line of their offerings. These are often trade or service marked to become their sole property.

Cold Calling

A salesperson's visit or telephone call to a customer or prospective customer without an appointment, advance notice or invitation. Often used as a prospecting technique to develop new sales leads.

Collaborative Marketing

Where two or more complimentary business entities or professionals work together on a particular product, service or promotion to the benefit of each. This enhances the strength and reach of each partner beyond their individual capabilities.

Collection Account
A charge account which has become overdue and submitted to a collection staff, agency or attorney for collection.

Collection Agent
One who hires out services to assist a creditor to collect past due receivables for a fee. These services are contracted for harder to collect balances and the fees are structured accordingly.

Collection Letter
A letter sent to overdue accounts reminding the account holder that payment has not been received and is in arrears. Usually one of several such letters, each becoming increasingly demanding of payment and explaining consequences and charges for past due accounts.

Combination Quotas
Sales quotas based on two or more factors with weights assigned to each factor according to relative importance. Often used as a guide in evaluating the salesperson's performance.

Comic Strip Advertising
The use of cartoon drawings in a comic strip type of situation or story sequence for advertising products and services.

Command Line

The headline or opener in an advertisement designed as the attention getter. Typically shown in bold typeface or with other style to gain the reader's attention over competing advertisements.

Commercial

A term used for advertisements on television or radio, and purchased for specific time periods or programming schedules.

Commission Merchant

A broker having goods in possession or directly under control until delivery is complete, upon which a commission is paid for services rendered.

Communications Mix

The various vehicles used in the transmission of a promotional message. The goal or desired end result will dictate the appropriate mix.

Comparison Advertising

A promotional strategy to feature an organization's products and services, as they compare to the competition, through advertising messages. This method can be successful, but must be done carefully to avoid retaliation or consumer backlash.

Competitive Advantage

An advantage one competitor has over others in the same marketplace. This may include location, product line, quality, value and pricing, for example.

Competitive Analysis

A survey and analysis of who are the current competitors in a given market or a given product or service line. An important resource in designing marketing strategy is knowing the competition.

Competitive Bid

A price quotation for a specific project or purchase according to known specifications. A competitive bid process is entered into by invitation. Some organizations require competitive bids for purchases over a specified dollar amount.

Competitive Parity

A measurement of the amount of money spent on advertising products or services in a given market compared with competitors in the same market.

Competitive Shopping

Shopping the competition's facilities or products to gain an insight into their prices, promotion, displays, customer service, sales practices and related factors. "Shoppers" should be trained people who know how and what to look for, possibly requiring an outside contract.

Complaint Handling

How an organization handles complaints is highly important to its success. Bonafide complaints must be handled quickly and fairly. An unrealistic complaint can be a tough call, but wisdom suggests giving the customer the benefit of the doubt.

Conceptual Testing

A form of market test in an attempt to determine if a given idea has enough merit to justify proceeding to develop it for the market. Often, a pilot test will be the next step before advancing too far.

Conditional Sale

A sale or an agreement of sale that is conditioned on some factor or event. This may represent a legal review, a make-ready preparation or conditioned upon approval of financing.

Confidence Level

In the sampling of a given population for a research survey, for example, it is important to know if the sample is valid, with a given degree of confidence. By statistical analysis or a confidence interval table it is possible to determine the sample size necessary to provide a given level of confidence. Researchers will typically look to achieve a confidence level of 90 - 95%. This means, for example, that if the required size sample for a confidence level of 95% was drawn from the same universe 100 times, it would be representative of that universe 95% of the time. See Reliability.

Consensual Validation
An informed reaction by an individual to consider the opinions of others while making a decision, such as a purchasing decision. This validates the importance of referral sources, satisfied users and testimonials.

Consignment
An arrangement whereby merchandise is delivered to an authorized agent for sale on a commission basis. The seller receives the sales proceeds less the consignment commission.

Consumer
The person who uses the purchase object and to whom significant marketing activity is directed. It is important to realize that the consumer may not be the same person as the purchaser. This is particularly important in purchases involving kids and the elderly.

Consumer Behavior

The buying behavior of the purchaser of goods or services, including how and why one purchase decision is made and others are not.

Consumer Mood

The state of mind of consumers at the time of a promotion or sale. Important to the advertiser because it may have a bearing on reaction to a particular message. Also an important factor in personal selling where the mood will play a role in how well the salesperson and the presentation are received.

Consumer Panel

A group of consumers selected to assist in the evaluation of products and services, be they new, improved or those of competitors. Panels are selected to serve for a single purpose or for a given period of time during which they may participate in a number of evaluations.

Consumer Panel Diary

A diary used by a selected panel to record responses to specific requests in evaluating products and services. The diary may be used in conjunction with a panel sitting or taken home to make various observations over time and recording them.

Consumer Profile
A demographic representation of consumers in a given geographical area or of particular products or services. The profile may be enhanced to include psychographic characteristics, as needed, and can be a valuable tool in developing marketing strategy. See Customer Profile.

Consumer Price Index (CPI)
A cost of living measurement by the Federal government to reflect current economic and market conditions. Also called the inflation index or cost of living index, it is reported on a monthly schedule. Often used as a guide in the pricing of goods and services in the marketplace.

Consumer Surveys
Research surveys for the purpose of gaining greater knowledge about a market in terms of demographic, geographic, economic or psycho-graphic characteristics. See Customer Surveys.

Contingency Planning
Making allowances and alternatives for unforeseen developments within marketing and strategic plans. Commonly supported by contingency funding through reserves or out-of-pocket payments.

Continuity Advertising

A series of advertisements each emphasizing particular aspects of a product, service or company. The same or different media may be used for the same series. The goal is to create an on-going or building interest by the target audience.

Control Group

An isolated data source that can be watched as a control, having known and constant variables, and used to compare to an equal or larger test group where variables are not necessarily known or constant. Provides for a measure of assurance that a particular test was a valid or representative one.

Controlled Association

A survey research method that helps limit the response to a specific subject, item or set of items. While the type of response sought may not be closed-end, there may be a desire to limit the number or range of responses to a select group or list.

Controlled Recognition

In survey research, refers to a respondent's choice from a limited list of items in a recognition survey for measuring advertising effectiveness or product association.

Convenience Products
Frequently purchased products that require little investigation and comparison shopping. These are typically minor food products and household items.

Cooperative
An association of providers or consumers formed for the purpose of reducing processing and handling costs or obtaining volume discounts in the purchase of various goods and services.

Cooperative Advertising
A joint promotional venture designed to provide a single message or offer. This can include wholesaler and retailer or similar combinations where the parties gain from the united presentation and shared expense.

Copy Platform
The basis on which to launch an advertising campaign or promotion, using unique qualities or special features of new and improved products or services. The message or tone of the advertisement is built around the copy platform.

Copy Testing
Researching a media message for effectiveness by means of interviewing a sample of the actual or projected audience. Recommended for testing

copy prior to actual media placement, the advertisement is typically placed in a "dummy" publication to give it real life-like surroundings.

Copywriter
One who writes copy for advertisements and promotional messages within specific guidelines provided by the agency or the client.

Core Product
The principal product object or benefit for which the purchase is made to satisfy a consumer's particular need. Additional features may reflect value added, but not essential to the purchase choice.

Corollary Data Reference
The use of sales data of a given product or service in determining the potential market for a related product or service.

Corporate Image
A public perception of a particular organization based on corporate direction and consumer reception. The degree of disparity between the corporation and the public image provides for both marketing challenges and opportunities.

Cost-Benefit Analysis

A study of the relationship of projected benefits of a product, service or program versus the anticipated cost of that effort. Benefits may be subjective, depending upon who will benefit. Costs will include design, manufacture, delivery and promotion.

Counter Cards

Poster display placards for desks and countertops used as advertising reminders or instructions to customers. Often consisting of a pocket or tray to hold "take one" fliers.

Coupon

In marketing terms, a coupon is an offer of a special purchase opportunity typically within a given time frame. Offers can include reduced price, two-for-one sales and trial offers, for example.

Cover Position

High profile advertising locations on the cover pages (inside or outside) of newspapers and magazines.

Crash and Burn

Jargon used to describe a totally unsuccessful promotion or campaign. The promoters realize early on that it is not going to work as planned, and decide to cut off life support.

Creative Advertising
A unique and imaginative approach to the design and message of advertising and promotion for a product, service or program.

Creative Selling
A unique and imaginative approach to the design of a sales strategy for a product or service. Sometimes certain customer types require an unconventional approach to achieve and retain their interest.

Credit Check
A review of a customer's financial background and credit history with special emphasis on current debt, repayment patterns and net income.

Credit Scoring
A formulized method for gaining a sense of a customer's credit worthiness. Consists of a list of weights assigned to particular credit qualities, income sources, obligations, household information and the like. These are totaled for a comparison to firm tolerance measures. Newer forms use computer models, allowing the inclusion of more variables.

Critical Path Method (CPM)
A project scheduling mechanism for controlling more complex objectives. Using a project flow diagram, time and complexity of key tasks can be factored in to provide for more effective monitoring of each step.

Cross-Sell
The tendency of particular products or services to be sold or used in conjunction with others offered by the same provider. Known cross-selling patterns can be used in designing marketing and sales strategy.

Cue Card
In survey research, a cue card is sometimes used to provide choices or ranges by which a respondent can select from a list for controlled recording of each such question.

Cumulative Discount
A quantity discount based on purchases over a specific time period used as an inducement to buyers to purchase more of a given product. The more purchased, the greater the discount factor becomes.

Curb Appeal
How things such as storefronts, window displays, architecture or motor vehicles look from the street as seen by typical or select passersby.

Customer Base
The list or file of active and recently active customers of an organization. The gross list may also contain sub-bases by marketing areas or customer types.

Customer Profile
A demographic representation of customers of a given organization or its products and services at a point in time. This can be a valuable tool in designing marketing strategy and advertising messages. The profile can be enhanced by including psychographic characteristics.

Customer Relations
An organization's active management of its relationship with current and prospective customers. A key to successful customer relations is to put customer service as a priority in marketing and sales strategy.

Customer Satisfaction
The degree to which the purchase of a product or service meets the expectations of the customer. If the purchase meets or exceeds expectations,

satisfaction is achieved. Otherwise there will be a degree of dissatisfaction, possibly leading to customer loss.

Customer Service Index (CSI)

A scale by which to measure the results of a specific customer service strategy. Creation of a fixed scale allows for measurement of degrees of success from one period to another, and for use in future marketing strategy.

Customer Surveys

An organization's research efforts to gain important information about its customer base in terms of demographic, geographic, economic or psychographic characteristics at any given point.

Customer Value Analysis

A test conducted to rate specific benefits customers value, and in what proportion to other benefits, for use in designing products, services and promotional materials.

Cut Throat Pricing

A price setting maneuver aimed at reducing or eliminating competition by reducing prices so substantially that there is little, if any, profit to be gained. Typically a short term strategy.

Cycle Billing

A method of staggering the billing of customer accounts over a month long period, according to an alphabetical or statistical selection process. This is typically done to spread out the billing and collection workloads for staff.

D

Database Marketing
Systematic collection, analysis and storing of customer and prospect information used to provide for more effective promotion and sales efforts.

Debit Card
Similar to a credit card in that it can be used for purchases, a debit card draws directly from the customer's bank account. This has a cost savings benefit for the retailer compared to credit card transaction fees assessed by issuers.

Deceptive Advertising
Promotional messages that include false and misleading statements or claims about products, services or the organization itself in an attempt to attract more customers. This is not a prescription for longer term customer loyalty.

Decision Theory
Statistical and computer modeling techniques used in the study of decision-making, as in the selection of goods and services for purchase, based on the interaction of select interrelated variables. These variables are essential to form consumer opinions and choices.

Decline Stage
A stage in the life cycle of a product or service in which sales begin to decline. This may result from a variety of factors including the onset of functional obsolescence, new products introduced into the marketplace and other corporate priorities.

Defensive Advertising
A reactionary advertising maneuver aimed at protecting business and position in the marketplace by attempting to counter competitive marketing practices.

Demand
Consumer want of goods or services in relation to the ability to pay for them.

Demand Expansibility
The expansion of demand for a product or service by increasing the number of customers without changes in price or customer purchasing power.

Demographic Analysis
The compilation and study of the vital statistics of a given market, using factors such as age, sex, marital status, income, household status and the like. Important information required for the development of sound marketing strategy.

Demography

A field of study focusing on population characteristics including age, sex, occupation, ethnic composition, density, location and size, for example.

Dependent Variable

In marketing, a consumer or opinion variable that is altered due to a change in an independent variable. Such variables may include demographic and psychographic characteristics, for example.

Depth Interview (also In-depth Interview)

An extensive personal interview in which attitudinal and motivational factors are examined, in addition to collecting vital statistics.

Derived Demand

A demand created by the introduction of a new product or service for which there are various support needs. A new piece of equipment may produce a demand for servicing that equipment, for example.

Deseasonalization

The process of computing and removing seasonal influences or variations from time series data, as in reporting by weeks, months or quarters, for example.

Detail Person
One who supports the sales effort but does not ordinarily sell. Instead, the detail person helps to influence sales by delivering brochures, samples and the like.

Dichotomous Questions
Survey questions with only two possible answers in an effort to force a response. A yes or no choice is one such example.

Differentiation
A marketing strategy to distance a product, service or organization from the competition in a given area by developing or focusing attention on differences or unique qualities of market offerings.

Direct Action Copy
Advertising copy designed to produce immediate reaction from the consumer audience. This includes announcements of sales for defined periods, trial offers and time sensitive coupon offers.

Direct Mail
Advertising and promotion sent to a specific list of present or prospective customers, by mail, within a given market. Mailings may include items such as letters, promotional materials and literature, samples of products, brochures and response coupons.

Direct Marketing

Business development by means of direct contact with customers and prospects. This may be accomplished by means of a company sales staff or hired independent representatives.

Direct Marketing Association (DMA)

A marketing trade association providing members with services and support in the promotion and sale of products and services. Educational and legislative support is also available to members. Headquarters: 1120 Avenue of the Americas, New York, NY 10036-6700.

Disclaimer

A statement printed on a product, package or service brochure providing the conditions or results for which the manufacturer or provider is not liable.

Discretionary Buying Power

Net income not allocated to the purchase of necessities by the family or individual spending unit. Sometimes referred to as discretionary income.

Display Advertising

Advertising in magazines, newspapers and similar publications that is customized using a combination of words, pictures, colors and size in an effort to gain reader attention.

Disposable Income
Net income remaining for consumer spending after all income taxes and required deductions have been taken out.

Divergence Analysis
An analysis of an organization's performance, such as in sales, versus that of competitors', with a desire to identify, improve and capitalize on identified differences.

Diversification
Expansion of a business into a new line of products or services. May be developed from scratch or acquired through merger, acquisition or partnership. The goal is to broaden market base and opportunities for growth.

Dog and Pony Show
A term typically used in reference to a presentation and all of its supporting graphics or displays, delivered by one or more people to a company audience.

Dogs
Products or services that have outlived their appeal and usefulness. May still generate some measure

of return, but are not worth significant marketing effort.

Door Hanger
A flyer or a plastic bag holding a flyer, small newspaper or product samples that has a hole used for placing over a door knob or handle.

Door Openers
A token gift given by a salesperson as a means of gaining entry to or the attention of potential customers in order to make a sales pitch. A means of gaining immediate attention and a willingness to listen.

Double Page Spread
Two pages of newspaper or magazine that face each other and are used for product or service advertising for one organization. The organization may be prominently featured as well. Also called a center spread.

Downsizing
A process by which an organization initiates an expense cutting plan through staff reduction or program cuts in an effort to improve bottom line performance.

Draw
The relative pull of a promotional message measured for future comparison with other messages, time periods, markets or media.

Drive
The sum of stimuli internalized by the buyer which induce a purchasing decision.

Drop Dead Date
The date at which time a particular message or offer ends. The date selected may be a calendar date, business day date or date of postmark.

Dry Run
A test or rehearsal of a sales presentation or other presentation for an internal or external audience. Used as a means of practice before the real thing.

Dual-Use Packaging
Packaging which has a consumer demand in addition to the contents of the package, used to boost sales of the product itself.

Dummy Magazine or Newspaper
A mock-up of a magazine or newspaper, arranged as it might appear, used for advertising testing purposes. The desire is to produce a real life appearance for the most effective testing.

Dunning Notice

A collection letter or form used to prompt payment for a past due account balance. Typically a series of such notices or letters are used with increasingly demanding language to generate action. See Collection Letter.

Durable Goods

Also called hard goods, these are such things as furniture, appliances and other home equipment typically sold in the retail market.

E

Early Adapter

Term used to refer to consumers who are quick to adopt new products and services coming onto the market. This group is second only to innovators which is the first consumer group to be attracted to new innovations in the marketplace.

Early Bird Sale

A special promotion that offers attractive discounts to the first customers arriving to the sale.

Easy Money Market

An expression used when there is a relaxation of lending restrictions and interest rates by lending institutions.

Economic Indicators

Data assembled from key business activity that are significant enough to have an influence on business activity, consumer behavior and action by governmental agencies. Examples include employment data, consumer price index and money markets.

Elasticity
An economic term reflecting the degree to which the supply or demand for products and services will change as a result of changes in price structure.

Electronic Marketing
Marketing of products, services or programs by such electronic means as the Internet, auto response systems by telephone and data entry terminals. The information is collected to produce a data base for future marketing purposes.

Elderly
A term formerly used to reference those now known as seniors. People 85 years of age or older are commonly referred to as elderly.

Elevator Bulletin
Advertising messages appearing on the inside walls of elevators in commercial buildings. These are relatively inexpensive, but with a limited captive audience.

Emotional Appeal
A promotional message that is designed to appeal to the consumers' emotions in an effort to persuade them to purchase specific products or services.

Empathy

In advertising, promotion and sales, this is an ability to project one's self into an actual or created situation in order to appreciate the customer's perspective.

Endless Chain

A method of obtaining referrals from referrals as a continual source of sales leads. Can be kept up as long as the effort to ask for new referrals continues.

Endorsement

In marketing, the use of an authority figure in the promotion of products or services can produce a desired affinity to a defined segment of the market.

End User

The customer who last buys and uses a given product. Distinct from suppliers and distributors, for example, in that these providers make purchases for resale rather than end use.

Emporium

Typically a large marketplace offering a variety of merchandise for sale. This may represent a single operator or a series of leased stalls or kiosks.

Entrepreneur
One who owns and operates his or her own business, and has the ability to keep it viable.

Environmentalism
Organized movements of concerned citizens and local, state and Federal agencies directed toward protecting and improving environmental conditions. The corporate marketing effort must understand the potential impact of these movements on the marketplace.

Escalator Clause
A clause in a contract for the sale of goods and services stating that a higher price may be charged if material increases in the cost of production or shipping occur during the course of the contract.

Ethics
A quality a person in business must strive to maintain in order to rise above temptation to provide less than the fairest of interpersonal relations in all their business affairs.

Ethnic Marketing
The marketing of products or services to specific minority groups or nationalities. This typically involves the use of select language and customs in an effort to draw the desired consumer group.

Exclusive Distribution
Limiting the number and location of dealers and distributorships, for control purposes, by means of exclusive rights. This is generally a legal business strategy as long as it does not create a restraint of trade in a given market.

Excuses
Less than sincere objections to a sales presentation. Instead of saying they simply do not want the product or service being sold, the prospect gives excuses as to why they cannot buy.

Exposure
The placement of advertising for products, services or programs in front of the potential market by means of various media outlets. A marketing goal is to maximize the number of times the average potential customer has an opportunity to see the message.

Expressed Warranty
A producer's guarantee that its merchandise will hold up under certain specified conditions and over a given time period or the company will make a suitable repair or replacement to the customer.

Extended Customer
Term used to describe the customer and others such as friends, family and advisors who may have a role in a person's purchasing decisions.

External Data
Research material that is obtained from sources outside one's own organization. Survey research and governmental statistics are typical examples.

Extra Dating Period
Implies that payment discounts are good beyond the initially specified date, at the seller's option.

Extrinsic Reward
A reward or gain received for doing an act unrelated to the reward itself. This may occur in interpersonal or commercial relations.

F

Fact Sheet
A form of publicity release giving the necessary facts and background to an editor or writer for producing a final copy.

Factors
A term used for commission merchants. Also a term for those who purchase an organization's accounts receivable at a discount and assume responsibility for collection.

Fad
A relatively short-lived product or service that temporarily catches the public interest. The market appeal rises quickly, peaks early and declines fast.

Fallback Position
A salesperson's maneuver when it becomes apparent they will not be able to make the full sale of a product or service as they had hoped. In an effort to salvage something a partial or lesser sale is pursued.

Fallout
Credit or bank account closings experienced shortly after a give-away or special promotion

ends, usually indicating the account was opened simply as a means to obtain the premium offer.

Family Brand
A group of products or services a provider promotes collectively as well as individually in order to gain maximum consumer acceptance for all of them.

Family Life Cycle
The distinct stages a family unit passes through as its members mature over time. These include a single member, married (with and without children), empty nesters and surviving spouse, for example.

Family Unit
A unit as defined by census analysis consisting of a head of household and others related by blood or marriage and living together.

Farm Out
The subcontracting of certain jobs to outside vendors by an organization for expediency or specialized workmanship.

Fear Appeal
An advertising message that produces a consumer reaction of fear if they do not act to a particular

appeal, whether the message was designed with that purpose or not.

Fear of Rejection

Salespeople will not be able to succeed if they are unable to get past negative responses from customers and prospects. They must be able to accept rejection as a part of the job, and work to offset the negative response or move on.

Feedback

Response to a message or promotion which can be used by an organization to determine reach, effectiveness, criticism and ideas for improvement. Such feedback may be requested or voluntary, and can be a valuable marketing tool.

Feeling Tone

Used to describe the good or bad feeling experienced by someone exposed to a specific message or advertisement.

Field Force

A team responsible for gathering primary data in a research project. The group may include staff members or contracted agents.

Financial Marketing

The marketing of financial services by banks, credit companies and other related institutions in addition to financial advisors and planners. The marketing of stocks, bonds and mutual funds are also included.

Finder's Fee

A fee paid to a third party for bringing together buyer and seller in a sales transaction. The fee may be paid by either party, depending on which one is taking the initiative in concluding the transaction.

Firm Price

A price fixed at a certain point and unaffected by fluctuations in market conditions.

First Cover

The outside front cover of a magazine, newspaper or similar publication. Also called the front cover, it typically contains a heading, cover photos, principal story headlines, date and price.

Flameout

Term used to describe an unsuccessful advertisement, promotion or campaign. The resulting response failed to meet expectations, necessitating premature termination of the promotional vehicle.

Flat Rate

A per unit charge that remains constant, regardless of the quantity purchased. Typically used for smaller orders or one of a kind items, where the seller has greater control over the transaction.

Flier or Flyer

See Circular.

Flip Card

See Cue Card.

Floor Plan

Inventory of a merchant financed by a bank or the manufacturer. Generally rates are favorable enough to be offset by sales of a more extensive inventory.

Focus Group

A selected group of usually 6 to 12 people used for in-depth discussions on advertising, promotion or products and services. A focus group is led by a trained moderator for best results. The group is not to be considered a fully representative sample of a given market.

Follow-up Call

A second or return sales call following a previous one, or a call in response to an inquiry by telephone, postal mail or e-mail. The call will typically reiterate a sales offer and respond to questions. The caller also will attempt to gain some sort of commitment from the prospect for further follow up.

Follow-up Letter

A letter sent following a sales presentation or offer, usually reiterating the discussion that took place along with additional information or incentives for encouraging action. Also may be used to respond to requests for additional information.

Forced Sale

A sale made according to a judgment in law by a court or some other mandatory requirement without consent of the owner. Goods sold in this manner may be sold at auction or by a receiver.

Forecast

A prediction of future performance based upon past performance and the best supporting information available. Forecasts are usually produced for a specific time period, e.g., annual, semi-annual, quarterly, or monthly.

Formal Balance

An equal or weighted physical measure of copy and pictures in an advertisement.

Format

A term applying to the basic elements of a publication such as size, shape, printing style, style of content and general appearance. May apply to broadcast media as well.

Fourth Cover

The back of the last cover of a magazine or newspaper publication, representing a prime advertising spot. Also called back cover or last cover.

Frame

A section in a cartoon or pictorial sequence used for certain advertising messages. Also a single picture in a film or video sequence.

Franchise

A licensed business arrangement where an organization or individual has an exclusive right to use plans, materials, logos and names in a given geographical territory for franchise or royalty fees.

Free Association

A research method that allows respondents to make their own associations in response to questions with little or no direction or limitation by the interviewer. The respondent is typically asked to say what first comes to mind after each interview prompt.

Freebie
A give-away premium used to encourage a purchase or open an account. May have the name and logo of the provider printed on the item given away.

Frequency Discount
A price break provided to frequent repeat purchasers of given products or services. This is a marketing strategy aimed at increasing customer loyalty.

Front Cover
See First Cover.

Full Line Forcing
A manufacturer's requirement that its distributor, wholesaler or retailer carry all or none of its product line. This can take the form of an exclusive dealership.

Full Position
Premium advertising space or location in newspapers and magazines, usually at the top of the page or next to reading material.

Full Run
Placement of advertising messages in all editions of a newspaper or periodical in an effort to maximize coverage for a given time period.

Functional Discount

Discounts given in return for special agreements, such as carrying larger stocks of products or certain product lines, and promoting them.

Fungible Products

Refers to products and resources that are consumed by use, but can be reproduced such as farm products, energy and fuel products.

G

Galley Proof
A pre-publication or printing of typeset publications and advertising materials for final review before actual use. Provides for an opportunity to make last minute adjustments and corrections.

General Line Sales Representatives
Salespeople who work with a wide variety of products or services and are responsible for knowing the available varieties, but not necessarily the specifics of every one.

Generic
A no-name or no brand named product sold as a substitute for the original. Generic products, including generic drugs, are priced lower due to savings on promotional costs. The quality of generic products may vary from brand names.

Genuine
For products and services it's the real thing and nothing less. In sales it represents a true and sincere desire to look beyond the sale and establish a lasting relationship with the customer.

Gen-X or Generation-X

A labeled consumer group including those born between the mid 1960's and the mid 1980's, sometimes referred to as children of the prior group which is labeled as "baby boomers," including those born between the mid 1940's and the mid 1960's.

Geographic Segmentation

The breaking up of a marketing area according to geographic sub-areas providing for more efficient analysis, promotion, sales and delivery operations.

Geriatric Marketing

Marketing goods and services to the senior market. A term less used in favor of senior marketing. This market typically has an age range of up to forty years or more, from say, age 60 to over age 100.

Gift Card

A card or announcement sent with a gift, often used with premium gifts designed as sales incentives, typically carrying organizational and individual names and logos.

Gift Certificate

A coupon type insert in a mailing or publication as an inducement to purchase a particular product or service or used as a thank you for a prior purchase.

Also may be purchased and given by individuals in place of a gift, representing a traffic builder for the retailer.

Gimmick

A token premium or other device used as an attention getter aimed at gaining the attention of potential customers to the message or promotion being offered.

Give-Away

A premium or freebie given to encourage a purchase or open an account. May include the name and logo of the provider printed on the item given away.

Glue Sealed Method

A technique used to determine magazine readership by examining whether or not glue seals between pages are broken. This is typically done through house-to-house interview and inspection of the magazine itself.

Goal

An integral part of an objective, breaking it down into one or more goals designed to achieve that objective. A goal may be further broken down into specific action plans.

Going Rate Pricing
A market strategy of basing product or service pricing on that of competitors, rather than cost plus margin or market demand. Generally this is shortsighted strategy or one for a special purpose over a given period of time.

Going Price
The current market price at which a good or service may be bought or sold.

Good Faith
In marketing relationships, it represents honesty and sincerity in dealing with customers in the conduct of business transactions.

Good Will
In corporate terms, represents the intangible assets of the company built up over years of good public relations. In individual terms, such as in personal contact, represents an interest in the contentment of others.

Grabber
An opening statement or offer in an advertisement designed to quickly spark the interest of the reader or viewer.

Grace Period
An automatic or selective extension of time allowed for payment of a bill or loan beyond the original due date.

Greeting
In sales, the greeting of a prospect will have a lot to do with the success of the presentation, as the first impression is so important. This is the first personal step in the sales process.

Grid Card
See Rate Card.

Gross Sales
The total amount an organization charges for its products or services over a given time frame, usually reported on a quarterly, semi-annual and annual basis.

Group Sales
Marketing and sales strategies must be developed to appeal to both individuals and groups of individuals. The group approach needs to take into account group dynamics in purchasing decisions.

Growth Stage
After introduction of a new product or service, the organization hopes for the growth stage, in the life

cycle of a new offering, where sales begin to increase rapidly.

Guarantee
A carefully worded statement designed to demonstrate a manufacturer's or provider's willingness to stand behind their products and services, and under what conditions.

Guaranteed Position
A contractual commitment that certain advertising copy will be placed in the same space in future editions of a magazine, newspaper or similar publication. A fee is charged for this exclusive positioning.

Guarantor
One who will provide a guaranty of someone else's performance under an agreement, such as in a credit or loan transaction. If a borrower fails to meet required terms, the guarantor may be called upon to do so.

Gutter Margins
The space on a printed page which is adjacent to the binding of a book, magazine or similar publication.

H

Halo Effect
The presence of unrelated or undesired factors influencing the interpretation of research data potentially damaging reliability of results. This tends to result in respondents giving higher or lower ratings to products or services because of the influence of various features, qualities or perceptions.

Handbill
Similar in design to a flier or circular, with printing on one side, and designed to be posted on a wall or handed out on the street.

Hard Goods
See Durable Goods.

Hard Sell
A bold or overpowering sales pitch often used repeatedly to gain a quicker response, positive or negative. If positive, move ahead to close the sale. If negative, move on to the next customer. Not a prescription for building lasting relationships.

Harmony
The blending of the various ingredients in an advertisement such as typography, color, rhythm, shapes, etc.

Hawker
A peddler of newspapers or merchandise who typically sells his wares outside a business establishment and on street corners.

Headline
Words or phrase used on the front page or headings on stories in a newspaper, magazine or similar publication. Usually set in bold print and an attention-getting manner.

Head-on Competition
A competitive rivalry among companies offering similar goods and services, each attempting not to be undersold.

Head-on Position
Placement of outdoor billboard and sign advertising directly facing oncoming traffic.

Healthcare Marketing
Marketing of health related products and services to a ready, willing and able market. Such offerings may be directed to organizations serving this

market or directly to consumers of such products and services.

Hedging
A process used to reduce risk of loss and protecting investments by diversification. This can be a designed marketing strategy.

Heterogeneous Market
Market conditions under which consumer demands are dissimilarly structured.

Hidden Offer
A special offer or promotion that can only be found by reading the copy of an advertisement. This can be an effective means of advertising testing.

High Pressure Sales
The salesperson persists in prevailing upon the customer to purchase with the hope that they will give in to the pressure by saying "yes," as opposed to relationship selling.

Hit List
A form of prospect list detailing who are candidates for a sales call, sometimes arranged by the potential each listing represents.

Holding Company

Two or more corporations assembled under a parent corporation for the purpose of expanding marketing operations while reducing operational costs.

Home Delivered Services

Products and services that are delivered directly to the home. These tend to be particularly important to senior and disabled customers.

Homogeneous Market

Market conditions under which consumer demands are similarly structured.

Honor

In a business transaction it is to meet the terms of an agreement as agreed, such as at maturity in a credit arrangement, or performance to specifications in a contract.

Hooker Opening

Used in advertising to describe the opening line "attention getter" in an advertising message.

Horizontal Integration

Expansion of operations by means of acquiring, or adding by other means, increased production, new outlets or branch offices of the same line of business.

Hot Prospect
A qualified sales lead that holds promising potential, and generally deemed to be ready, willing and able to buy.

House Organ
A company's own news publication for the benefit of its employees. Properly designed, these can also provide marketing opportunities.

Household Unit
A unit living together, related or unrelated by blood, with a primary head having an income and place of residence, as defined for census recording.

Huckster
An independent salesperson, such as a peddler or hawker, who combines sales technique with entertainment, sometimes with an edge of trickery.

Hype
Special promotional efforts to call attention to a program, organization, product or service where there is a need for quick attention.

Hypothetical Question
A means of analyzing or critiquing something by trying to create an assumption of an actual situation. This can be a meaningful exercise prior to the launch of a promotion or event to anticipate public relations.

I

Ice Breaker

Often used at the onset of a sales presentation to start a conversation on a lighter note, a salesperson may open with comments about the weather, a sports event, current events or something of interest known about the prospect.

Idea Generation

In a healthy organizational environment, ideas for new products, services or programs, or improvements in them, are readily encouraged. This helps keep management and staff challenged, and the organization well positioned in the marketplace. Idea generation requires a well managed screening process.

Image

The collective attitudes opinions and perceptions the market holds for a particular product, service, brand or company. The goal in advertising is to capitalize on this knowledge in the design of promotional messages aimed at image creation.

Implied Copy

In an effort to broaden copy appeal, advertising messages sometimes contain statements made to create impressions, in the reader's or listener's mind, favorable to a product or service being promoted. Often such messages are accompanied by various disclaimers in small print or rapidly spoken words.

Implied Warranty
Unwritten or unspecific warranty on products and services implied because of the type and conditions of the sale, but usually governed in law by virtue of the intent.

Impression
A consumer reaction to products, services or programs. The goal is to measure consumer reaction, in an effort to create a most favorable impression.

Impulse Buying
Unplanned purchase of items which are decided upon during the course of purchasing other items, often highlighted by point-of-purchase displays.

Inactive Account
An account relationship that remains open, but without recent activity. Marketing decisions such as how long to keep an inactive account open, and how to reactivate these accounts need con-sideration.

Incentive

An inducement aimed at getting customers to make a purchase. It may come in the form of a small gift, a coupon, a contest or reduced price, for example.

Incentive Program

A motivational effort aimed at staff and hired sales agents to increase new business development and customer retention over a given time frame.

Incorporation

The process of forming a corporation, including preparing a corporate charter and by-laws, and filing within the state of corporate registry.

Incremental Analysis

A research method used to estimate the audience or appeal change at various price and perceived value levels in decision-making situations.

Indemnify

To make good on an obligation of another against loss or damages by means of reimbursement or other consideration.

Independent Variable

In marketing, a key consumer variable that may influence or cause a change in another variable, and alter values and opinions. These variables may include demographic and psychographic characteristics, for example.

Index Method
Used primarily for sales measurement purposes, it is a process of distributing a total sales forecast among territories or sub-areas by select factors.

Indirect Action Copy
Advertising copy not specifically designed to produce an immediate sale, but rather used for creating favorable impressions or good will.

Indirect Advertising
Advertising brand rather than product or service. Also, advertising a given product or service that indirectly relates to another.

Indirect Questioning
A research method used to obtain information from a respondent by asking questions about related factors or situations, in an effort to direct a respondent's attention to the focus of the survey.

Inducement
Any act or incentive aimed at moving a person to action. In sales, inducements may be used to convince a prospect to consider a purchase.

Influencers
Within the organization, influencers help provide direction in decision-making and setting the course. In the marketplace, individuals in family units, buying groups, extended customer friends and relatives, professionals and advisors can play a significant role in influencing purchasing decisions.

Infomercial
A trade term for an expanded advertising segment of paid programming. Longer and more expensive than a standard commercial, these promotional presentations can last for 15 minutes to an hour or more.

Informative Advertising
Advertising messages specifically designed to inform potential customers about a new or improved product, service or program. The desire is to create an early demand.

Informed Choice
A purchasing decision made with essential information at hand. The buyer has acquired, directly or indirectly, the necessary information to satisfy any pre-existing doubts.

Inherited Audience
A media audience, usually in radio or television, that is left over from a previous program or production.

Innovation
A new product, service or program believed by consumers to be a new offering in the market place. Those who are first willing to try it are considered to be innovators.

Innovative Marketing
A conscious organizational effort that encourages and challenges staff to consistently strive to be a market leader in the development, improvement and marketing of its products or services.

Innovators
Consumers who are the first of a group willing to test or try a new product, service or program. They are willing to do this without the benefit of it being time-tested or improved through use.

Input
A person's reaction or ideas surrounding a given issue that are actively sought by a producer or marketing researcher.

Inquiry

A sales lead that may come directly from a prospective buyer of a product or service. An inquiry is made to get information and that begins the sales process.

Inquiry Test

Returns from a coupon or mail promotion examined for a specific purpose. This is a common technique for advertising testing purposes.

Insert

Promotional material included in an advertising flyer, a package of merchandise, a billing statement or a newspaper, magazine or similar publication.

Installment Charges

The financing charges periodically assessed on payments made over the life of a credit card or loan balance.

Installment Purchase

A purchase made on time for the extension of credit from the retailer or a finance company. Typically, used for larger purchases such as automobiles, furniture and appliances.

Institution
An organization or corporate entity created for a public good, typically through the provision of services, such as healthcare and support programs. These organizations have marketing needs as well as more corporate entities, and are typically non-profit operations.

Institutional Advertising
Promotion of the organization rather than its products or services, or promotion of a particular industry of goods or services. Sometimes called trade advertising.

Institutional Sales
An area of sales directed to non-commercial accounts, including the healthcare industry, education and various public service organizations.

Integrated Commercial
Use of a product or service which is blended into the program itself, and is consistent with sponsorship of that program.

Integrated Marketing
A promotional program where various vehicles are used to produce a more coordinated marketing effort. This may include advertising, public

relations, direct mail, point of purchase materials, and personal contact, for example.

Intent
What a person means to convey, whether by words or actions, which may not be consistent with how it is interpreted by others. This is an important consideration in the design of promotional messages.

Intermediary
An individual or organization that plays a role between the manufacturer or provider and the customer, commonly known as a middleman role, such as a sales representative or delivery service.

Internal Data
Research material that is available from within an organization's existing files and records, and not available to outside sources without permission.

Interpolation
A statistical estimation of a value falling between two known values in a specific table or other listing of values.

Interpretation
A process of evaluating the response to a particular product, service, program or promotion through the use of various research methods.

Interrogation Headline
An advertising headline that asks a question in an effort to get the reader involved in the copy. Also called an interrogating headline.

Interval Recording Scale
A scale of equal intervals used for recording degrees of preferences, motivations, attitudes, meaning and the like. One such example is the semantic differential seven scale measurement technique.

Interview
A formal inquiry by a researcher or another who desires to assess reaction to a product, service, program or promotion by means of a survey questionnaire.

Intra Vires
Powers within the given authority of a corporation in law. See Ultra Vires.

Introduction Stage
The life cycle stage for a product or service where the offering is first made available for sale in the marketplace.

Introductory Offer
An invitation made to the consumer where their willingness to try a new product or service will be

rewarded by means of a discounted price, a free gift or similar consideration.

Irritation Association

A brand association test for various remedy products, where the researcher attempts to measure a brand's remedy association versus other brands or other remedies.

Island Display

An arrangement of merchandise in or near a customer traffic pathway, separate from other merchandise. This may include special discount products, trial offers or close out merchandise.

Island Position

An advertisement that is surrounded by reading material or blank space, but not other advertisements. Provides for reducing surrounding clutter and is usually a more costly position in a newspaper, magazine or similar publication.

J

Jargon
Unique phrases that develop within an organization or industry that are germane to that group, but unfamiliar or possibly misunderstood by outsiders.

Jingle
In marketing terms, a more repetitive, short rhyming musical verse designed to support the promotion or advertising theme for a product, service, program or organization.

Jobber
A business operating as a middleman, buying from wholesalers and selling to retailers. Also frequently coming under the category of distributor.

Job Shop
A business that produces products or materials to the order of others. These are typically smaller operations, often sole proprietor, that respond to orders rather than producing on speculation of business to come.

Joint Ownership
Possibly growing out of a joint venture that moves to an ownership position for the partners, or any

business that is created by control and ownership of more than one investor.

Joint Sales Call

When two or more sales personnel make a call on a customer or prospect. This is commonly done when there is a need for an expert present, such as an engineer, to explain technical details. Joint sales calls are also used in training new sales staff.

Joint Venture

A partnership agreement between two or more entities designed to take advantage of a marketing opportunity not necessarily attractive or feasible for either of the partners alone.

Judgment Sampling

A sample selected according to someone's judgment rather than by statistical methods, based on personal experience, historical information or a degree of familiarity with the subject material sufficient to maintain objectivity.

Junk Mail

A negative term used to describe direct mail advertising and solicitation sent unsolicited to a commercial mailing list or other database.

Juried Research

A research technique whereby products, services or promotional materials are rated or ranked according to the weight of opinion of a consumer panel or jury.

Jury Panel

A consumer panel of a smaller number of individuals brought together to discuss products, services or promotional material, as directed by a panel moderator, in an effort to gain insight helpful in future marketing strategy.

Just Price

A price placed on goods or services that is realistic relative to market conditions, and what an informed buyer would be willing to pay.

Just Value

A realistic value placed on a product or service by the consumer relative to market conditions and market acceptance.

K

Kaleidoscopic Packaging
A packaging strategy in which the producer attempts to create consumer demand for the package as well as the package contents. Re-useable containers are one example.

Key Account
An important marketing relationship, based upon past and potential new business, that an organization must continually strive to preserve as an active customer.

Key Area Evaluation
An internal evaluation of corporate management in terms of areas such as marketing, productivity, profitability, resources, financial condition, manager performance and such other areas as the corporation chooses.

Key Marketing Area
A principal area for the marketing of goods and services that an organization covets for developing business. More often a greater proportion of the marketing budget will be allocated to this area of opportunity.

Keyed Advertisement Coupon
Marking a coupon with a special code to determine its origin in a particular magazine, newspaper, mailing or location. This provides support for advertising decisions based upon known response sources.

Kickback
A payment given in return for a business favor generally not covered by contract or company policy. Many forms of kickbacks are unethical or illegal in nature and frowned upon as a business practice.

Kicker
An added feature to a sale or contract designed to enhance the marketability of the offer. This may include associated services, warranties or other added benefits to that offer.

Kick Off
The beginning of a new promotional campaign for a new or improved product, service or program. Also may signal a special offer or other special event.

Kill Date
A drop dead or end date for a promotional message or special offer after which previous terms and conditions no longer apply.

Kiosk
A free-standing booth, counter or display area typically in a shopping mall or area where smaller retail operations are conducted. The vendor benefits from smaller rent charges and the facility owner benefits by adding to rentable retail space.

Knee-jerk Reaction
A quick response to some form of stimulus without thinking before reacting. In marketing, this can negatively effect sound practices for reacting to marketplace challenges.

Knock-Off
A lower priced replica of a successful brand name product, often produced with lower priced labor and materials, designed to capitalize on the ready made market for the original.

Knowledge Base
The accumulation of information and expertise an organization has available to help solve marketing and operational issues or other challenges.

Known Probability Sample
A statistical sample in which the relative probability of each unit being selected is a known factor.

Kudos

Recognition, both formal and informal for a job well done. May be accompanied by a material gift, plaque or some form of incentive award.

L

Label
The name, logo and certain descriptive information on a product package or the product itself, used as a means of identification. Common colors, print styles and design help provide familiarity and consistency.

Last Cover
See Fourth Cover and Back Cover.

Latent Defect
A defect in a product sold, possibly unapparent to the seller, but undetectable to the buyer.

Launch
The introduction of a new product, service or program to the market, typically accompanied by a promotional campaign to provide a successful introduction.

Law of Diminishing Returns
In marketing, repeating direct mail to the same market may yield results, but over time at a diminishing rate. The same holds true in sales, where the number of calls on a given group of prospects will yield diminishing returns.

Lay Away Plan
A program designed to increase sales by offering the buyer to select goods to be held, pay for them on time and receive them when the full price is paid.

Lead Generation
Promotional or sales activity designed to produce new sales leads for follow up by sales and support staff. Leads may come from a variety of sources including current customers.

Leading Indicators
In marketing terms, leading indicators are known signs of the potential business climate over a given time period. These are identified by historical company data and local, regional and national business indicators.

Leading Question
A question, such as in a marketing research survey, that is worded in a way to suggest a specific response or direction. Unless this is by design, it will likely bias the response and survey validity.

Leaflet
A folder, circular or brochure designed as a self-mailer or to fit in a standard #10 business envelope. Leaflets are designed to be used for

direct mailings, personalized mail or "take one" displays.

Letter of Credit

A commercial instrument issued by a bank or other financial company for a fee which serves as an inducement to securing a specific transaction or loan.

Letters Patent

A formal document issued by a governmental agency granting a right or privilege to an individual for the conveyance of title to a property.

Level of Confidence

See Confidence Level.

Leverage

An organization's use of its assets and influence to further its business goals. When assets are encumbered with debt, the amount of leverage will be lessoned proportionately.

License

A contractual agreement providing an organization or individual permission to use a specific property right, under specified conditions, in exchange for a fee or royalty.

Life Cycle
A series of changes people pass through in the course of their lives where their needs and means continually change. A valuable source of information for designing marketing strategy for select audiences.

Life Style
A style of living usually dictated by one's age and means, although not necessarily a strict rule. Some people may live beyond their means or outside their life cycle for short periods of time.

Limited Warranty
A warranty on a product or service that contains specific conditions clearly spelled out to limit liability.

Linage
A measurement of space in newspapers and magazines used primarily for pricing advertising. A page is typically measured by the number of possible printed lines.

Line of Credit
A credit limit applied to a customer's account allowing for purchases and payments over a given time period, according to stated limitations.

Liquidate
Settlement of an obligation by agreed upon terms, sometimes by court order. Upon closing a business, a liquidation sale may be held to dispose of assets. Proceeds may be used to settle claims of creditors.

List Broker or Merchant
An organization or individual providing mailing lists for rent or commission. These lists are of vital importance to direct mail campaigns and can be selected by various demographic and geographical breakdowns. Often such lists are one-time use per fee.

List Price
A retail price for merchandise as recommended by the manufacturer or distributor. The retailer may choose to price below list price as a purchase inducement.

Lobby Survey
A research survey conducted in the lobby or reception area of a business establishment, used for getting on-the-spot customer interviews. While not statistically valid, these types of surveys do provide street-side opinion and curb appeal reaction.

Local Brand
A product produced or handled by local establishments carrying a local or regional brand name. The local appeal provides for promotional efforts aimed at supporting local merchants.

Logo
A unique representation of a company's trade name or brand, using personalized lettering and symbols designed for promoting recognition in the marketplace. This provides for promoting brand awareness and brand consciousness, as well as consistency in the marketplace.

Loss Leader
A product or service sold at near cost or below to attract customers in anticipation that they will purchase other items. Used primarily as a traffic builder to get the customer's attention.

Low Balling
An ill-advised tactic employed by a salesperson where the quoted price is lower than the actual price in an effort to generate traffic. The customer is then convinced to "buy up."

Low Pressure Sales
A sales strategy that employs a more subtle approach to making a sale, recognizing the longer

term value of establishing a relationship with the prospect.

Loyalty Program

A marketing incentive designed to retain customer business through special offers, discounts or association by membership. Examples include frequent flyer and frequent purchaser programs.

M

Magazine Coupon
Coupon offers found within magazine publications providing a marketing opportunity to selectively reach a targeted audience. Such coupons are typically coded to identify their source magazine.

Mail Order Sales
A means of selling by direct mail, catalog or direct response where business is transacted through postal and private delivery systems. The seller may or may not have a location open for walk-in business.

Mail Panel
A consumer panel similar to a jury panel, but run by mail correspondence. Often larger than a jury panel or focus group, and used over a longer period of time, providing for an ongoing dialog.

Mailer
Commonly known as self-mailers, a flier, circular or brochure is designed to fold or provide space for a mailing label so that the piece is dual purpose.

Manufacturer's Brand

A product, service or corporate brand developed and owned by the manufacturer or provider. These are more often national brands, as opposed to regional or local brands, but this is not universal. Branding costs can be substantial.

Margin of Error

See Reliability.

Margin Pricing

Pricing products and services by averages in an effort to estimate an average contribution to total margin. This is often used when separate products or services are in large numbers.

Marginal Account

A customer relationship where the sales volume is barely sufficient to keep the account profitable. The organization must decide at what point the account is no longer viable, and take necessary action.

Marked Down Sales

The sale of merchandise where the price has been lowered, usually because of inventory surpluses, end of the line products or a closeout.

Market
The potential demand for specific goods or services in a defined geographical area. Can be further refined by demographic and other analysis.

Market Challenger
A leading competitive organization that is working hard to increase its market share at the expense of the competition.

Market Demand
The sum total of customer interest in particular products or services in a specific market area over a given time frame and marketing environment.

Market Development
An organization's effort to build business demand in a given demographic or geographic market, or to expand its present market coverage.

Market Drift
The shifting of geographic or demographic market segments due to uncontrollable causes, such as urban renewal, suburban growth, traffic and transportation pattern changes and governmental decision making.

Market Follower
As opposed to a market challenger, the market follower desires to hold to its market share while

content to let competitors lead. The hope is that the more aggressive competitors will compete with one another for growth.

Market Grids
An expression in table form of market information for a particular product or service. Information used includes product or service by type or grade, geographical area, and form of distribution.

Market Leader
An organization, product or service that possesses the largest market share in a given industry or area. A leader of this type typically leads the way in new product/service development and promotional efforts.

Market Niche
See Niche Market.

Market Penetration
Represents a share of a given market, be it geographical, product or service. Typically expressed in percentages, this is a marketing strategy for growth by means of increasing sales in a specific market area.

Market Position
The relative status of a product, service or brand compared to the competition in terms of price,

quality and reputation. This is a marketing strategy to reach a desired place in a given market, for products or services, relative to competitors in that market.

Market Potential
The total quantity of products and services that could be sold in a given area under optimum market demand.

Market Price
The pricing of goods and services according to current market demand. Sometimes referred to as "going price," meaning what the market will bear.

Market Profile
A description of the characteristics of a given demographic or geographic market. This detail provides the basis for developing marketing strategies.

Market Research
A systematic examination of a pre-determined demographic, economic or geographic market, in an effort to determine potential marketing opportunities prior to product, service or market development.

Market Segmentation
The process of breaking down the total market into smaller, but similar units or sub-markets according to specific factors such as demographic and psychographic characteristics.

Market Segments
Sub-markets of a larger, more heterogeneous market separated by affinity to provide for a better understanding and exploration of total market composition.

Market Targeting
A process of identifying the most attractive place or segment in a market for a given product or service at a point in time.

Market Test
A pilot test to a sample market of consumers to measure and evaluate new or improved products, services and marketing campaigns.

Market Value
The value in price a product or service has such that it can be sold at any given time, and the market accepts and is willing to pay that price.

Marketable
Goods, services and financial instruments that can be quickly sold or transferred to a market that is ready, willing and able to purchase.

Marketable Title
Title to a property that is unencumbered and can be promptly transferred to a ready and willing buyer.

Marketer
A professional employed in any of the marketing disciplines, including management, research, sales, promotion and direct response marketing.

Marketing
An organized process of promoting the flow of goods and services most conveniently and effectively to the customer at a profit. Profit may be measured in net monetary return or the achievement of a specific goal in the process of realizing a monetary gain.

Marketing Area Analysis
The study of a given geographic market area for business development or expansion in terms of population, spending power, competition and other potential opportunities.

Marketing Audit

A comprehensive review of an organization's marketing performance relative to a benchmark standard. These periodic reviews might be carried out by a carefully selected internal team from areas other than marketing, or externally by an independent organization.

Marketing Concept

A management goal driven philosophy representing a commitment to satisfy a given market demand at the optimum profit, and to do so more effectively and efficiently than its competitors.

Marketing Control

An important function of the organization is to periodically measure and evaluate the results of action plans for marketing strategies in an effort to see if the goals and objectives have been achieved.

Marketing Dynamics

Forces influencing the business climate within which the marketing function must operate. Internal dynamics include those the corporation must face in terms of available resources, expertise and commitment. External dynamics include the present nature of the entire marketing environment.

Marketing Intelligence

The marketing research function is responsible for collecting and analyzing information about the marketplace that can be used in designing and implementing marketing strategy, as well as evaluating results.

Marketing Mix

The various feature components of marketing that are available for application to a particular situation or market condition. Commonly including product, price, place and promotion, and also known as the four P's of marketing.

Marketing Plan

A written document detailing the marketing objectives, goals and action plans for the organization over a given time period. This typically is part of the organization's annual business plan.

Marketing Research

A systematic process of developing, collecting, recording and analyzing facts and figures from a given market for a specific marketing purpose.

Marketing Risks

Risks in the marketplace caused by man-made acts or acts of nature which might be confronted in any marketing effort. Marketing research is the means to mitigate many forms of controllable marketing risks.

Marketing Strategy
A set of objectives developed by the organization, as part of its marketing plan, for its products, services or programs.

Marketplace
A specific location or geographical area where particular goods and services are sold. This includes, retail shopping districts, open markets, or wherever there is an assembly of potential customers.

Mart
A term used to refer to a marketplace containing a number of sellers operating under one roof or contiguously.

Masked Identification Test
A research method used to test the respondent's recognition of a brand or product without the name being revealed.

Masthead
The official label of a newspaper, magazine or other publication which may contain titles, logos or both.

Matched Samples
Two or more samples matched by pairs or groups frequently used for testing sample adequacy.

Mathematical Model
An expression of a theory of a situation in mathematical terms for the purpose of applying statistical analysis.

Matrix
A display of numerical values in a grid or bracket arrangement used in problem solving where there may be several unknowns.

Maturity Stage
In the life cycle of a product or service, a point will be reached where sales growth begins to level off as demand slackens. This is commonly referred to as the maturity stage.

Mediation
A dispute resolution process sometimes used in extreme customer relations situations. A third party mediator may be called upon to help resolve outstanding issues. The goal of the mediator is to achieve as close to a win-win resolution as possible.

Media Mix
The various forms of media available to project a message, including print media, radio, television, billboards, direct mail and the Internet, for example, in the development of promotional messages and advertising.

Media Penetration
The share of household units a given message reaches in a pre-determined area, quantifying the value of a specific medium or media.

Mental Set
The attitude or mental state of a respondent before and during a survey interview. This is important to know as it could have significant bearing on the response(s) given.

Merchandise
Ordinary goods sold to the public, commonly associated with retailing.

Merchandising
Process of marketing goods and services most efficiently and effectively in terms of price, timing, place, size, quantity and quality to meet the needs of the customer. Often associated with retailing, effective merchandising requires bringing together the promotion, the goods and the

necessary mix of salesmanship in order to be successful.

Merchant
One whose business it is to buy and sell merchandise, typically buying at wholesale prices for larger quantities and selling piecemeal at retail prices.

Merchantable
Goods that are of such a quality as to be suitable for sale, and comparable to similar goods found in the marketplace.

Merchantable Title
See Marketable Title.

Message Mix
The use of various media available to transmit a message or promotion within a given market area for a particular purpose.

Methodology
The orderly approach and means used in obtaining the solution to a problem. In a structured environment, methodology is recorded and documented for future reference.

Metropolitan Statistical Area

See Standard Metropolitan Statistical Area (SMSA).

Milline Rate

The cost per agate line of one million copies of an advertisement in a magazine, newspaper or similar publication.

Mission Statement

The organization's statement of purpose and overriding objective in its operating environment.

Missionary Salespersons

Specialty salespeople used by manufacturers to call on wholesalers in an effort to get them to move specific products. These are sometimes good will calls.

Mock-up

A model or other representation of a product used in advertising design and the sales process. Mock-ups may be required if the actual product is not portable or if the product is yet to be produced.

Model Building

An expression of ideas and relevant facts relating to marketing and economic activities, in mathematical terms, often computer generated.

Used as a tool in designing marketing strategy by means of simulation.

Mom and Pop
Derived from small family owned stores, this term has become a reference to most any type of small retail or start up business.

Monopoly
An economic situation in which there is but one supplier in a given market and thus, an absence of competition.

Moral Consideration
An obligation that may not be legally binding, but based on commonly accepted ethical standards is reasonable to expect others to do under similar circumstances.

Motivation Research
Research directed to an analysis of "why" people act or react to given stimuli. What makes consumers respond the way they do to given stimuli is an essential marketing strategy building need.

Motivator
A person, an offer or other factor that motivates someone to react in some way. Also important in

the sales process for an idea of what is likely to motivate a prospect.

Multiple Correlation Analysis
A statistical approach to determining market factors using more than one of a select group of independent variables, usually displayed in graphic or diagram form.

Multivariate Analysis
The inclusion of several variables, which cannot be isolated from one another, in a market analysis. The approach will require statistical analysis to measure the relative influence of one variable at a time while holding the others constant.

Mystery Shopper
A technique used to stimulate sales personnel by offering a reward for successfully handling an imitation customer who is actually rating the salesperson's performance. Mystery shoppers are usually independent contractors or services, and less likely to be picked out of a crowd.

N

Name Brand

A brand of product or service well known over a larger geographical area that is marketed for its brand name as well as its product or service identity.

Name Recognition

The extent to which a brand, product, service or organization is readily identifiable by consumers in a given market, measurable through survey.

Narrative Copy

Advertising copy written in the form of a story as a means to hold the reader or listener's attention.

National Association of Manufacturers (NAM)

A large U.S. industrial trade association established to promote competition, standard of living improvement and be conducive to economic growth. NAM offers an array of advertising sponsorships. Headquarters at 1331 Pennsylvania Avenue, N.W., Washington, DC, 20004-1790.

Need

A necessity that a person has to have in order to live day-to-day. Food, water and shelter are common examples of need categories. See Want.

Need Recognition

Recognition of need is the first stage or step in the buyer decision-making process, where the prospective buyer recognizes a need to be satisfied.

Need Satisfaction Theory

A theory applied to sales stating that if a need can be identified, people will respond to satisfy that need through a purchase. A necessary application in the design of sales strategy.

Negative Appeal

An advertising approach that focuses on the ramifications of what may or may not result if a particular product or service is not purchased.

Networking

A concerted effort to meet and get to know sources who can be of help in identifying new business leads for staff and the organization. In the process of gathering referral leads, it is possible to keep filling the need for new referrals by getting leads from leads.

Niche Market
A smaller market for a specialized product or service where the number of potential customers is relatively low, but provides sufficient potential to justify a marketing initiative.

Non-bleed
Where printed material or advertising copy provides for a white or plain margin border to set it off from other copy, thereby reducing clutter interference.

Non-cumulative Discount
A quantity discount on specific items and orders used as an inducement for buyers to purchase larger quantities at one time.

Non-durable Goods
See Soft Goods.

Non-profit Marketing
The promotion of the goods or services from public service organizations providing programs for community benefit and charitable purposes.

Non-response Bias
A bias that can develop in research surveys because certain respondent types do not respond, creating a lack of representation within the total sample, and possibly questionable results.

Non-verbal Communication

In sales, the salesperson needs to know the importance of other than verbal communication. Things such as body language, gestures, silence, appearance, hand shake and timelines say a great deal about interest and sincerely.

Normality of Data

The extent to which a distribution of data is normal and forms a typical bell curve when presented graphically.

Noted Score

An advertising testing measurement of the total number of readers who reported having seen or heard a particular advertisement.

O

Objections
Issues raised by a prospective customer in the course of a sales presentation that the salesperson must overcome in order to proceed. These may include price, style, color, size, timing and need, for example. An objection may be raised as an excuse not to buy rather than having to say "no."

Objectives
Part of a strategy or other plan. With an objective in mind, specific goals and action plans can be developed to ensure the likelihood of success. In sales, each sales call should have predetermined objectives.

Observation Test
The study of a group of people exposed to a particular message, product, service or promotion to gauge their initial physical and mental reactions. A form of observational research.

Observational Research
The process of collecting, tabulating and analyzing primary data obtained from observing targeted groups of consumers in a given market.

Obstacles
Barriers confronted by the salesperson in the process of attempting to make a sales presentation. These are temporary or permanent barriers including timing, change of health or monetary status, or even death, for example.

Offer
In marketing terms, an offer is a proposal for costumer consideration. In exchange for a commitment, special terms for acquisition may be made available. Special offers may provide reduced prices or premiums in exchange for purchase.

Offer Testing
A trial by survey of an anticipated promotional offer. The testing may involve an offer price, reduced price or an offer premium.

Oligopoly
An economic situation where there are only a few suppliers in control of a given market.

Omnibus Advertising
The advertising and promotion of several unrelated products or services at one time in one advertisement. This may include the products or services of one or several companies, possibly coordinated by an independent promoter.

One-On-One

Another term for a face to face encounter, as in a sales call. This is the most direct contact possible, and the odds of success are greater than direct mail or telephone solicitation.

On-Line Shopping

Shopping for goods and services through a variety of Internet merchants. This has opened up new marketing opportunities, as there is almost no end to what can be sold on-line.

Open Account

An account that is currently active with a credit relationship. There may or may not be a balance due on the account, but there is evidence of recent activity. This provides an opportunity for direct mail and statement stuffers to promote new sales and special offers.

Open Advertisements

Advertisements that include the advertiser's name, telephone, address or web site, as opposed to a blind advertisement.

Open End Question

A survey question where the respondent is not provided with response choices or interviewer direction. Used in depth interviews for ferreting out opinions and feelings.

Opinion Leader

A person or group whose influence, through communication or behavior, serves as a model for the direction of others. Important in a marketing sense in that acceptance or rejection of products, services or programs may depend on the role of such leaders.

Opinion Rating

A survey tabulation based upon respondent opinion rather than fact. There is no right or wrong answer, but the opinion is important in evaluating products, services and promotional materials.

Option

An opportunity to purchase something within a given time period without fear of it being sold to someone else. An option may require some form of consideration for the privilege, such as a fee to be paid if the purchase is not made.

Order of Merit Method

A technique used in research projects as a means of allowing respondents to rank, by preference, a given list of items. Also called order of preference.

Order of Preference

See Order of Merit Method.

Order Taker
In sales, the one who takes an order, whether by telephone, by mail or in person. Often, the order taker does not sell, but acts as a support to sales.

Organizational Image
The manner in which an organization is seen or perceived by individuals, groups and other organizations in the marketplace. This is a consideration in the development of a corporate mission statement.

Outdoor Advertising
Billboards, signs, posted handbills and the like provide a unique opportunity to target promotional messages in specific markets or traffic areas.

Outlets
A retail store, sometimes owned by the manufacturer, that typically sells brand name goods at a discount. Such goods are sometimes over-runs, closeouts or imperfect items.

Outside Sales
Sales made by person-to-person contact outside an organization, retail outlet or factory made through the sales staff. A form of direct marketing.

Overhead

Non-operating expenses associated with running a business. Utilities, insurance and real estate taxes are typical examples of overhead expenses.

Overkill

In marketing terms, the excessive promotion of a product or service beyond the potential return or market forbearance is considered overkill.

Oversold

Sometimes a sales presentation can oversell the product or service to the point of talking the prospect out of a purchase. This emphasizes the need to know when to ask for the sale, and that is not necessarily at the end of a presentation.

Over-The-Counter

Products sold to the public through retail outlets without pre-qualification. Non-prescription drug products are commonly referred to as over-the-counter drugs.

P

Package Insert
Materials included in the packaging along with the contents. This may include information and directions about product use, or may be marketing oriented offering additional products, coupons or special offers to the buyer. Demographic surveys are sometimes included, as well, which can be used in future marketing initiatives.

Package Merchandising
The planning and design of merchandise packaging in an effort to increase sales appeal of the contents of the package.

Packaging Concept
Marketing consideration given to what a package should look like and what it should do for helping sell the contents of the package.

Packing Slip
A form memo included with or in a shipped package of merchandise, detailing what is to be found in the package. This is used as a check on contents for both shipper and recipient.

Paid in Advance

Where a purchase of goods, services, or subscriptions are paid before receipt of the purchase. This usually is done in exchange for a reduced price since there will be no billing or credit balance to collect.

Painted Bulletin

An outdoor billboard advertisement painted on the sign board, as opposed to those papered.

Paired Comparison

A research technique that asks respondents to select preferences from various pairs of items rather than a simple list. By process of elimination it is possible to arrive at an accurate ranking of individual items, as well as the relative relationship between items.

Panel

An advertising panel is a term sometimes used in reference to a billboard. Also see Consumer Panel and Jury Panel, which are research groups.

Participating Sponsorship

Two or more advertisers joining together to sponsor a program, message or cause. Benefits to be gained include achieving greater coverage with fewer dollars, and the potential advantage of association with another organization.

Partnering
A relationship between organizations, formal or informal, where there are mutual benefits for marketing, production or sales. May be an extension of the networking process, and may provide opportunities for future joint ventures.

Party Plan Sales
The sales of products by means of invitation, typically hosted by a relative, friend or acquaintance of the invitees. A company representative makes a presentation to the group and takes orders. Samples are shown and often refreshments are served.

Patent
A grant of exclusive rights to a product design by the U.S. Patent Office, providing for ownership and the right of use reserved to the owner.

Patent Applied For
Wording put on products and product packages indicating that a patent is in the process of being reviewed, but not yet granted by the U.S. Patent Office.

Patent Pending
Wording put on products and product packages indicating that a patent has been approved and is in

the process of being registered by the U.S. Patent Office.

Patronage
An important follow-up goal in the sales effort is to build lasting relationships. A thank you note or telephone call can go a long way to encourage customer patronage for future business.

Pawnbroker
A business operator who lends money on the collateral of personal property pawned in his shop.

Payment Mechanism
A payment option provided the customer for satisfying an obligation. This may include cash, credit card, debit card, charge account or any other means offered.

Peddler
An individual or independent contractor selling merchandise curbside, out of a motor vehicle or door to door. See also, Hawker and Huckster.

Peer Group
Generally an informal group of relative equals by age, social group, profession, skill set or educational standing. While making purchasing decisions individually, affinity to a peer group

may have an impact on the decision-making process.

Peer Pressure

This can have a positive or negative impact on sales. Customers may buy or not buy goods and services because of the real or perceived influence of their peer group. An important phenomenon for the marketer and the salesperson to understand.

Penetration

See Market Penetration.

Penny-Saver

A term used to reference local or regional display and classified advertising circulars and related publications made available free by delivery or pick-up. The words penny-saver may appear in the title of the publication.

Perceived Risk

What a buyer considers when making an unfamiliar purchase, and there is an assumption of the unknown because there is a lack of historical reference.

Percent of Sales Budgeting

Establishing a promotional budget based on a defined percentage of the sales forecast, or a percentage of the per unit sales price.

Perception

The basis on which an opinion on a product, service, program or organization is formed. This may result from firsthand knowledge or assumption, or through opinions from others, articles or promotional literature.

Perceptual Bias

In consumer research, a discretionary bias on the part of the audience toward a particular promotional message and what it offers the market, as measured by survey. Provides important material for developing promotional strategy.

Perquisites (Perks)

Incentives or privileges provided as an inducement to promote a higher level of achievement, commonly used with sales personnel.

Personal Influence

The degree to which certain people can sway the opinion of others toward promotional messages, products, services or programs. This is an important factor in marketing strategy and personal selling.

Personal Interview

A research survey that requires a trained interviewer to ask questions and record the responses on a survey form. Surveys may include both closed-end and open-end questions.

Personal Property
Movable properties, currency, negotiable and debt instruments, and various rights other than those pertaining to ownership in real property.

Personal Selling
Sales presentations requiring personal contact between the prospect and the salesperson. Contact can be in person, by telephone or personal correspondence, but there is a common goal to establish a relationship between buyer and seller.

Personality
A psychographic characteristic important to identify and explore by marketing research for the development of strategy for certain types of messages promoting products, services and programs.

Persuasion
The act of influencing behavior toward or against an idea, a message, product, service or program. This is an important factor in marketing strategy and personal selling.

PERT
See Program Evaluation and Review Technique.

Pilot Study
A conceptual test, by means of survey research, of an idea or prototype with a sampling of the potential market. The goal is to determine potential acceptance prior to actual development.

Pilot Test
An experimental test of a message, promotion, product or service prior to going public. This effort often uses real customers as a representative sample of the market. As opposed to a pilot study, here there is a test of what is being developed beyond the conceptual stage.

Placard
A display poster made to rest on a desk or counter with a particular message or set of instructions. May also contain a pocket or other container for "take one" literature.

Place
One of the marketing mix four P's, place is a marketing strategy that focuses on the market area, including the availability and convenience of obtaining the object of the marketing effort.

Planned Obsolescence
A marketing and production strategy where the goal is to produce goods that will wear out, before

the need for replacement, in an effort to capitalize on changing consumer demand.

Point of Purchase Display
Promotional signs and advertising displays that are near the checkout counter or other purchase points, promoting various products or services. Sometimes includes special offers or incentives. Commonly referred to as P.O.P. displays.

Ponzi Scheme
Named after Charles Ponzi, who promoted a famous pyramid type investment scheme in the 1920's, this is an illegal gimmick enticing investors with unrealistic returns. The system falls apart when there are not enough new investors to provide sufficient capital to pay all other investors.

Portfolio Test
Sample of advertising or promotional material shown by an interviewer to a select group or at random, by means of a portable folio or notebook, used to pre-test reactions to the material.

Positioning
A marketing goal of an organization to establish the most advantageous spot (position), relative to competitors, in the mental and physical marketplace for its goods and services.

Post Purchase Evaluation
In the purchase decision-making process, there is a point after a purchase has been made to satisfy a particular need or want where the purchaser mentally passes through an evaluation of the merits of what they have purchased.

Post Testing
The measurement through research of accomplishments compared to predetermined goals, such as marketing promotions, advertising messages, and program, product or service introductions.

Power of Attorney
A legal instrument providing for one person the right to act for another. Such an arrangement can have marketing implications in goods and services purchased for seniors. The user and the buyer may not be one and the same.

Pre-approach
The first and one of the most important steps in a sales presentation. This is the planning and preparation that must be done prior to making contact with a prospect.

Precision Sample
A statistical sample with a known degree of precision or confidence, where the margin of error

can be accurately measured. See Confidence Level.

Predatory Marketing

More of a cut-throat approach to out-market the competition, this is an attempt to take business away from competitors. Although usually a legal strategy, it can result in retaliation and more competition.

Preferred Creditor

A creditor who has a preferred position being entitled to payment before other creditors. A mortgagee is generally a preferred creditor.

Preferred Position

Specific locations or times in newspapers, magazines, radio and television media considered to be prime spots, and typically at a higher cost.

Premium

An incentive or bonus offered for the purchase of a product or service intended as a business builder. These may be used with new or improved offerings as a means of introduction.

Premium Promotion

A promotional campaign using certain premiums, prizes or give-aways as consumer inducements and business builders with new or improved products, services, programs or opening new account relationships.

Presentation
The act of making a sales pitch, including presenting all of the reasons to buy, showing examples, focusing on features and benefits and asking for the sale.

Presold
Customers who desire or know about a product before it reaches the market, and who may have already convinced themselves to buy, are said to be presold.

Press Kit
A public relations or news release packet usually containing a written press release, photographs or diagrams, biographical information and other factual materials. Typically used as an inducement to get a release or article published in newspapers and magazines. Kits are sometimes mailed to publishers, but are often given out during a public announcement.

Pressure Group
An organized group of people making an effort to exert an influence on political, social or economic developments. The strength of such influence may require attention in developing marketing strategy.

Prestige Marketing

Promotional efforts aimed at enhancing the image or public perception of select products, services, programs or an organization itself. This is sometimes coupled with higher-end pricing to help reinforce a prestigious image.

Presumption

Something logically assumed to be so based upon sound reason and past experience. Marketing is not all based on fact, and there are times when presumption is a necessary part of a process.

Pre-Testing

A research method of testing an advertisement, product or service, or promotional campaign on a market sample before going to the full market, allowing for final adjustments.

Price

One of the marketing mix four P's, price is a marketing strategy of attracting business through a lower price to undercut competitors, or a higher price to enhance the quality or prestige image of an offering.

Price Cutting

A sales strategy to either undercut the competition, increase traffic, or get rid of certain merchandise to make room for new offerings.

Primary Audience
The target market for a product or service promotional message that is selected based upon geographic, demographic and various other preferred qualities.

Primary Data
Information assembled for a particular purpose from sources such as files, reports, previous research data and informed sources from within the organization.

Primary Marketing Area
The strongest business development area within a targeted geographic market, justifying greater attention and resources from the marketing organization.

Primary Package
The material immediately surrounding the product. Sometimes this is a permanent container, and at other times a protective cover until the product is sold.

Principal
An item of highest rank or importance. In authority, one who is primarily responsible for a cause, debt or a loan balance.

Principle

A rule of substance or fundamentally sound such as in economics or the sciences, and one from which other principles may be derived.

Private Label

A contractual arrangement where an organization's name and the names of its products and services are put on goods and materials produced by others. Providers of this service have similar contracts with other non-competitive organizations in various markets.

Probability

The likelihood that something will or will not happen or that a statement or finding is true or false. Probability is a valuable marketing tool when certainty is not known or cost prohibitive.

Proceeds

Value in money or in kind received as payment in the exchange of real or personal property.

Product

One of the marketing mix four P's, emphasis on product is to concentrate on the design features and benefits of the product, rather than price, promotional value or the marketplace.

Product Development
A marketing strategy that focuses on developing new or improving existing products (services) as a means of building growth in a given market area.

Product (Service) Differentiation
Aspects of a particular product or service that can be advantageous to promotional strategies when identifying strengths over generally similar competitive products.

Product (Service) Life Cycle
The course of product or service life based on sales, profitability and corporate usefulness during distinct life stages including development, introduction, growth, maturity and decline.

Product Mix
The relative influence of various products produced and sold by a company at any given time. Service mix represents the same influence of service providers.

Profile Survey
A consumer survey that concentrates on the demographic characteristiscs of a designated group of consumers. More advanced profile surveys may get into select psychographic characteristics, providing for enhanced profiling.

Program Evaluation and Review Technique (PERT)
A systematic use of network techniques in project planning and control through a diagrammed display, providing for ease of access, review and process control.

Programmed Learning
A self-learning technique using a system of paragraph reading with select words left out. The reader (student) is asked to fill in the blanks from available information in each section's pre-reading material.

Projection
A statistical estimation of a value based upon an analysis of other data with known values and historical trends.

Projective Techniques
Using story telling, word association and other tests in an effort to identify hidden responses and meaning in marketing research. The goal is to get respondents into a particular simulation in an effort to evaluate how they might act and react in a real life situation.

Promo
Short for a sales or advertising promotion. May represent one message or more of a campaign

containing a series of messages, incentives, displays, contests and publicity.

Promotion

One of the marketing mix four P's, promotion is a marketing strategy that places emphasis on the development and placement of advertising and other promotion to build business. Often used for existing products, services and programs.

Promotion Mix

The formula designed to promote specific products or services in conjunction with marketing objectives. Such a formula may include advertising and other promotion, personal selling, publicity and public relations.

Promotional Allowance

A price reduction offered retailers for making a certain amount of stock purchases over a given time period and coinciding with a special promotion. The reduction may be offered by the manufacturer or supplier of the goods.

Prospect

A prospective customer identified for business development. The prospect may be obtained through direct mail, other advertising generating a direct response, or by referral.

Prospecting
The formal act of seeking out new sales prospects. This may be done through a variety of means including cold canvassing, networking or seeking referrals from existing customers.

Prospecting List
A list of sales prospects organized for efficient use by the salesperson. Typically more than an alphabetical list, but prioritized by potential and location, and possibly by known customer needs.

Provocative Headline
A challenging advertising headline that is intended to get the reader's attention and their desire to go on to read the message copy.

Psychodrama
A psychological role playing technique used to simulate consumer motivations, attitudes and behavior patterns in given situations. Used in advanced training exercises and to assist in developing marketing strategy.

Psychographic Segmentation
The classification of a market by such characteristics as social class, personality and lifestyle. Typically used to pinpoint marketing efforts to a more exact customer base.

Publication Profile

A demographic analysis of the readership audience of a newspaper, magazine, newsletter or other publication. Additionally, psychographic analysis may be used in audience profiling.

Public Corporation

An organization incorporated for public purposes, such as municipal governments, school districts, community owned utilities, and based on public service rather than a higher rate of return on investment to satisfy stockholders.

Public Relations

A marketing strategy using planned corporate publicity and customer relations in an effort to gain reception to a promotion, product, service or the organization itself. Allocating marketing dollars to the PR function may result in media publicity through press releases.

Publicity

A non-paid form of media promotional support to an organization and its products or services. Corporate publicity that is managed and paid for is often considered public relations.

Pull Strategy

A marketing strategy that relies on advertising and other promotion to pull in business from the marketplace. Coupons and other direct response vehicles are commonly used.

Pulling Power

The relative strength of advertising and promotional efforts in attracting business, i.e., pulling in customers for business.

Purchase Decision

The point or stage in the buyer decision-making process where there is a commitment to buy a given product or service.

Purchase Privilege

A customer offer to purchase an item at a special price with the purchase of another item at the regular price, while purchased at the same time.

Purchasing Unit

An individual, family or group living together, with a primary head, purchasing goods and services as a unit.

Push Money (P.M.'s)

A cash bonus given to salespeople as an incentive for selling particular goods or services within a special time and at a designated price.

Push Strategy

A marketing strategy that relies on a variety of promotional means to push products and services through the marketplace. Special displays and incentives are commonly used.

Pyramid

An illegal business or investment scheme that promotes unrealistic returns to attract new investors, but must use new investor money to support the returns of the other investors. Eventually the system falls apart as it becomes impossible to pay everyone. See Ponzi Scheme.

Q

Qualified Buyer
A customer who meets certain requirements of the seller, such as credit worthy, in addition to being ready, willing and able in all other respects to make a purchase.

Qualified Endorsement
A written endorsement designed to limit the potential liability of the person or organization offering the endorsement. Often used on negotiable financial instruments.

Qualified Lead
A prospect lead that has been determined a bonafide potential customer on the basis of a desired profile. Things such as age, marital status, ability to pay and authority to buy are typical considerations.

Qualifiers
Questions asked of potential prospects to determine if they are approved or qualified to be bonafide prospects for sales.

Qualitative Interview

A survey interview where the interviewer does not use set questions, but keeps the respondent focused in a general direction to cover certain subject matter. These are sometimes audio or video recorded for accuracy and future reference.

Quality

A standard of measurement by which a producer of goods and services measures output, and upon which the buyer measures performance of the purchase.

Quality Control

A formal process of inspection the producer of goods or services uses to measure consistence to fixed company standards. This can apply to what is produced and the marketing process, as well.

Quantitative Interview

A survey interview where the questions are formalized and structured to allow a set tabulation. Answers that can be response checked, as opposed to a narrative, are used allowing for manual or electronic tabulation.

Quantitative Methods

The use of mathematical techniques for the quantification of basic concepts and approaches in solving marketing problems. The key to precision is in the assignment of values to be used mathematically.

Quasi-contract
A contract implied in law rather than by specific agreement, and is a result of circumstances bearing legal implications.

Questionnaire
The form used in a research survey providing for the orderly flow of questioning of a respondent by an interviewer or self completion. Questionnaire design is also important for recording and tabulating survey results.

Questionnaire Disguise
Research questionnaires are sometimes disguised by using extra questions on a different topic as a means of preserving the identity of a company, product or service, and reducing perceptual bias.

Queue
A controlled method for the orderly movement of a line of customers in waiting, such as in a bank teller line or movie theater. Roped pathways are often used to maintain order.

Queuing Theory
A research technique employing mathematical probability analysis to the arrival and departure of

individuals in retail lines, teller lines and similar customer waiting situations.

Quid Pro Quo

Consideration given in return for something received, representing both tangible and intangible compensation. May represent an agreement to do or not to do a particular act.

Quota

A set goal for measuring performance achievement such as those set for a sales staff. The quota may be based on number of sales, dollars of sales or a percentage increase over a previous period.

Quota Sampling

A sampling method where the interviewer is assigned a specific quota of interviews to complete within defined parameters of respondent types, timing and geographical area.

Quote

A formal presentation of the price and other terms under which a vendor or contractor is willing to sell goods or provide a service.

R

Random Sampling
A statistical sampling method where every unit has an equal chance of being selected for a sample from a total universe or population. Reliability and confidence levels can be achieved by meeting sample size requirements per universe size.

Rapport
A communication and relationship building ideal to which a salesperson aspires in order to promote the best opportunity for a constructive sales presentation.

Rate Card
A card or sheet containing advertising rates and other detail for a given communications firm in the media market. Provides necessary information for planning advertising schedules and placement of ads. Sometimes referred to as a grid card.

Rate Differential
The degree of difference between advertising rates from one area or provider of services to another, typically based on volume. Also used to compare local and national advertising rate variance levels.

Rating Scale

A chart of values custom prepared and used internally and externally to rate an item such as an advertisement against a given list of criteria. The procedure can be repeated and provide a means for past and future comparison.

Reach

The coverage realized for a promotional message or a marketing campaign measured in numbers or percentages of people reached at a given point in time.

Read Most Score

In advertising testing, refers to the number of readers who read at least half of a given advertisement, out of a list or sample of other advertisements, and rated accordingly.

Readability

A measurement of how successfully advertising copy has achieved its objectives in an under-standable, readable manner. Respondents are asked to read copy and then asked questions to measure readability. Surveys sometimes ask questions of respondents about advertising copy they may have seen recently, without the benefit of re-reading it. This can provide an opportunity to measure retention, as well.

Reader Traffic
The number of people reading a given page in a particular newspaper, magazine, newsletter or other publication, as measured by survey response.

Ready Market
An existing consumer need for a new product or service which will require little business development. This may represent both new and improved market entries.

Real Property
The land and what is constructed on it, along with any rights associated with the property.

Reasonable
What commonly might be considered rational and consistent with good reason. Reasonableness is an important quality to both buyer and seller in a sales transaction.

Rebate
A discount in the form of a partial return of the purchase price under certain conditions, such as time frame, financing terms or by return of a coupon or proof of purchase seal.

Recall
The ability of a respondent to remember a particular advertisement or message, as measured

by survey research. What aspects are or are not remembered provide clues to the development of future advertising messages.

Receiver
A person appointed by court ruling to receive, protect and dispose of a property as directed by the court. The disposition may require marketing support to attract the most qualified buyers.

Reciprocity
An arrangement where there is an agreement to do or not do something in exchange for a favor in kind. This may be as simple as exchanging referrals or a more extensive agreement that may represent a potential illegal restraint of trade issue.

Recognition of Need
In purchase decision-making, this represents the point at which a consumer need or want surfaces that can potentially be satisfied through a particular purchase. The challenge for marketing is to discover how to create the best opportunity, through promotion, for such recognition to develop.

Recognition Technique
An advertising testing approach used to determine if respondents remember having seen particular

advertisements, as measured against seeing others in a publication or within a given period of time.

Recourse
A right by agreement to proceed against another who is obligated to make good upon the default of the one primarily liable. A guarantor is an example of such an obligated party.

Reference Group
A group, club or other association to which people belong or desire to belong because of prestige or common interests. Members and other associated individuals refer to the group as a means of behavioral direction.

Reference Price
A price a prospective buyer has in mind for reference when shopping for a particular product or service. This "price" may be based upon hard evidence, what is perceived or believed to be accurate information, hearsay or even wishful thinking.

Referral Lead
A lead provided through another customer or a business contact. These are especially valued prospects because they come with some pre-qualification and recommendation. See Endless Chain.

Refund Offer

A sales strategy that attempts to increase sales volume by means of an offered return of the purchase price if the customer is displeased. Similar to trial offer.

Reinforcement (Consumer)

An event or set of events that has the effect of strengthening the chance of a potential buyer making a particular response, such as whether or not to make a specific purchase. See Recognition of Need.

Rejection

In sales, this typically is a "no" response to an invitation to purchase in a sales presentation. The successful salesperson will know how to react, such as whether to come back at another time with a modified approach or to move on to the next prospect, as opposed to fearing rejection in succeeding presentations.

Relationship Marketing

A marketing strategy containing a sincere objective to build and maintain strong customer relationships in an effort to keep them for the longer term. The strategy must recognize that to keep these customers they consistently must be provided the value and service.

Relationship Selling

A proven sales approach where there is a sincere effort on the part of the salesperson to establish and build a relationship for the longer term. The goal is to work toward a relationship that will continue to yield new business, while maintaining customer focus.

Reliability

The degree to which one can rely on data developed through various research and statistical measurements, including marketing research and statistical sampling. The reliability for a given sampling universe will increase as the sample size is increased. Conversely, the margin of error will decrease. See Confidence Level.

Reminder Advertising

A concerted effort to place a brand or product message reminder in view of a given market. Typically, little more than the product or a slogan is used as reinforcement.

Rent Roll

A list of tenants and rents payable in a residential or commercial property. The rent roll is an important document in the transfer of real estate, application for financing or direct mail and statement stuffers.

Rep
Short for representative, such as in sales or a manufacturer's representative who may act as an agent for several companies, or as member of a company sales department.

Repeat Purchase
A sales strategy that offers an incentive for successive purchases of a product or service. Typically, a coupon is enclosed with the purchase to encourage the next purchase.

Replacement Guarantee
A guarantee that the seller or manufacturer will replace defective products without charge or on a pro-rated basis, often within a given time frame under specified conditions.

Replicated Sampling
Sampling the same population more than once to detect important influencing factors and potential bias. Used when sampling precision is of paramount importance.

Representation
A statement of fact or actions to that effect implying a truth or certainty. This can be particularly important in salesmanship where the words and actions of the salesperson may be taken as a representation.

Representative Sample
A sample that is truly representative of all characteristics and in their relative proportions to the total universe of units sampled.

Reseller Market
Purchases that are made with the intent to resell them to others representing a new market. Those who make such purchases for resale are usually wholesalers and distributors.

Respondent
The person who is being interviewed in a research survey, responding to questions asked. Respondents typically are part of a designed statistical sample or a specific location.

Response Constant
The amount of sales generated per advertising dollar at a specified sales level. Sometimes called sales constant.

Restraint of Trade
Agreements and other actions with a purpose of restricting fair competition, fixing prices or circumventing free trade activity. In most situations this is an illegal act.

Retainer

An advance payment or a contract for a service to be performed, such as a consultant or advisor, over a given period of time. The fee agreed upon is a constant whether or not the full service is required.

Retention

A marketing strategy that aims to retain a customer base by means of satisfying customers. Retention is a valuable asset in countering natural customer attrition through death, relocation and other uncontrollable factors.

Retrospective

A look back to events, data and other information from the past. Often this is an important exercise prior to the development of marketing strategy for promotion, research and sales initiatives, where an historical perspective can be helpful.

Returns

Products that are returned for a refund or equivalent credit under terms of the sales agreement. Sales returns represent a challenge for the company since they reduce sales, but may be a competitive necessity and a customer relations builder.

Revolving Credit
A credit plan allowing customers to make purchases and pay for the goods and services in monthly installments. Credit may be administered by the seller or through a finance company. Credit cards are a form of revolving credit when balances are carried from month to month.

RFP
Abbreviation for Request For Proposal used to solicit bids for professional support for specialized needs such as research surveys, advertising programs, sales training, legal representation and various consulting jobs.

Role Playing
A simulated situation used in sales training and survey interviewer training, using staff and professionals, where participants switch roles in mock exercises. Provides training experience while emphasizing the empathy factor.

Role Set
Formal and informal roles that are present at any given time in a group or association of individuals with which the group operates in performing its activities.

Rotation Advertising
The alternating of an advertising message by medium or message content in an effort to enhance reception.

Running Head
The repetition of a publication name or subject title in an article, book, newspaper or magazine appearing at the top of each appropriate page of the publication. Also referred to as the header.

S

S.I.C.
Standard Industrial Classification coding used for identification of industry and business types on a regional basis. A valuable asset in developing commercial and industrial marketing strategy.

S.M.S.A.
See Standard Metropolitan Statistical Area.

Sacred Cow
Something held in high regard that cannot be challenged. This may represent something of sentimental value, but not necessarily real value. A sacred cow may be more of a problem than an asset in business terms, because of its inflexibility.

Salable
Similar to marketable, a salable product or service is one that is fully ready for sale and has a ready, willing and able customer audience.

Sales Agent
A hired representative who has the authority to act on behalf of a seller. Usually the degree of freedom to act is controlled by means of contractual terms.

Sales Aid
The support tools a salesperson has in the sales kit to help make presentations successful. These may include demonstration models, visuals and incentives, such as coupons or samples.

Sales Campaign
A defined program designed as a business builder. It may be built around a theme or event, and well promoted to enhance the likelihood of success. May also include special incentives for the sales staff.

Sales Constant
See Response Constant.

Sales Conversion Rate
The rate at which contacts are converted into sales, expressed as a percentage. Number of sales ÷ contacts = conversion rate. Contacts may be by telephone solicitation or person-to-person sales.

Sales Decay Constant
A constant per cent decrease in sales each period in the absence of any advertising or promotion. Represents a decrease in volume of sales, as expressed in units or dollars, over given time periods. Serves as an aid in planning the phasing out of products and services offered in the marketplace.

Sales Development
A structured process of bringing in new business by various means, including prospecting, and supported by a coordinated marketing effort.

Sales Forecast
A projection of anticipated sales over a given period of time, based upon known historical information and the best market research estimates available. Economic conditions, competition, corporate priorities and sales training can all have an impact on how well forecasts hold up.

Sales Forecasting
The task of projecting future sales based on historical data, and related to known and anticipated market conditions.

Sales Incentive
Consideration given salespeople for exceeding a goal or quota. The incentive may be paid in the form of a bonus in cash, a special prize, or other gift of comparable value.

Sales Kit
The full set of sales aides at the disposal of the sales staff for their use in sales presentations. See Sales Aid.

Sales Objective

The basic result desired in a sales initiative, made up of a set of goals and specific action plans. The objective may be part of an overall marketing strategic plan.

Sales Penetration

The degree to which sales have been successful in a given market with a known potential. Success may be measured in dollars or percentages and recorded for comparison to historical and future periods. Also used to measure success against competitors in the same market.

Sales Presentation

In a sales call, the salesperson strives for the opportunity to present an offer of a product, service or program, along with all the details, in an effort to make the sale. This is commonly referred to as the presentation.

Sales Promotion

A coordinated marketing effort designed to build sales volume. This may include incentives for both customers and sales staff. Special offers, discounts, coupons, displays and staff incentives are common ingredients.

Sales Prospecting
Searching the marketplace for new sales prospect leads. This typically is done through networking for referrals, satisfied customers, cold calling and canvassing other possible sources.

Sales Quota
A management devised standard by which to measure the performance of the sales staff or a specific sales effort. Quotas may be set in sales dollars or percentages, and may be set by number of new accounts or calls made per period.

Sales Referral
A sales lead provided by an outside source such as current customers, business contacts or other networking for prospect leads.

Sales Triad
A group of three people in a selling situation where the salesperson needs to get a feel for the group dynamics in order to best make a sales pitch. The two other individuals may be related or unrelated.

Salutary Products (Services)
Basic products or services, without the "bells and whistles," but beneficial to purchasers over the longer term. Some insurance products can be categorized as salutary.

Sample
A marketing research term for a selected segment of a larger population or universe, as it is called, for survey purposes. The sample may be selected by a variety of sampling means, depending on the need.

Sample Design
A plan developed for the methodology to be used in selecting a sample from a specific data source or universe.

Sampling Precision
The reliability of a given sample and the consistency with which the sample can be replicated under similar circumstances and conditions.

Sample Reliability
The degree to which there is a minimum of sampling error or bias in sample data, sufficient to meet the needs of the sample purpose.

Sample Stability
The degree of difference measured as the sample size is increased and the deviations in the results decrease. An important factor in determining confidence level tolerance in relation to sampling cost.

"Satisfaction Guaranteed"

A manufacturer's or provider's guarantee to the customer that they will be satisfied with their purchase or they will be compensated in a stated way, such as their money back.

Saturated Market

A market condition where there is no longer significant potential for a product or service because of heavy sales penetration and competition.

Scaling

A research technique for ranking preference in a list of items by assigning a numerical rating scale, such as one to ten. Used to show degrees of preference in addition to straight ranking.

Scam

Not all marketing is in the best interest of the public. Unfortunately, sometimes "good" marketing is misdirected to produce a bad end, resulting in unsuspecting customers being duped or scammed.

Scare Copy

A form of advertising using fear as a motivation to promote a particular message in a given market. Not a universally acceptable approach, and it can be counterproductive.

Sealed Bid Pricing

Some cost estimates are requested by means of a sealed bid. This may result from corporate policy and to keep bids independent from one another. The challenge for the bidder is to set a competitive price, allowing for a favorable rate of return.

Season Dating

A method of delaying payment beyond the purchase date in return for an earlier order. This is used where a benefit to the buyer can be used to provide a benefit to the manufacturer or distributor.

Seasonal Discount

A reduced price for merchandise purchased out of season, such as clothing, gardening supplies and holiday sensitive items.

Seasonally Adjusted

An adjustment of statistical data used for the purpose of removing or decreasing the influence of seasonal fluctuations in business volume.

Search and Evaluation

As used in purchase decision-making, this represents the next steps after there has been a particular need or want identified. This begins the process of selecting a means to satisfy that need, including comparison shopping, searching advertisements and available literature, and talking to family, friends and associates.

Second Cover
The inside of the front cover of a magazine or similar publication, generally used for advertising purposes. Considered by advertisers as a prime location, and therefore more expensive.

Secondary Data
Information assembled from sources that presently exists somewhere outside the organization, such as in libraries, census data, annual reports and trade journals.

Secondary Goal
A target that is planned for, but is secondary to the achievement of a primary goal. Sometimes referred to as a sub-goal.

Secured Creditor
A creditor who has a preferred position, should the borrower default, by virtue of having their credit extension backed by some form of security or collateral. A real estate or mortgage loan, for example, is secured by the property itself.

Seen Associated Score
An advertising testing measurement that tabulates the number of readers who report having seen or

heard a particular ad message, and who were able to associate the message with a specific product, service or company.

Segmentation
The breaking down of a defined market into smaller units or segments by various demographic, geographic or psychographic characteristics. Used as an aid in the precision of marketing initiatives.

Selective Message Distortion
Promotional messages and advertising copy will not be heard and understood by everyone in the same manner. This may result in distortion of the original message, and may be passed on as such to others.

Self-mailer
A business reply form, folded postcard or brochure that is used in a marketing mailing, and designed for convenient postage paid return mail by the addressee.

Seller's Market
A market condition in which there is a shortage of goods or services for the existing demand. This provides the seller an opportunity to maximize the return on sales.

Selling Concept
An organization cannot sell enough products or services in a given marketing place without the support of a well defined, organized and executed sales and sales promotional effort.

Selling Formula
A canned approach to selling where a presentation is essentially memorized. The salesperson is not permitted much freedom to deviate from a script. This approach is typically used with new salespeople and on more basic products and services.

Selling Mix
Similar to the marketing mix, this includes the various disciplines of sales, such as direct sales, telephone sales, and sales by mail, for example. A company may employ any combination of the sales mix to reach sales goals.

Selling Process
The sales act itself, including all that must be done to achieve a sale. From preparation to follow-up, and everything in between, the process must adapt to the needs of each sales situation.

Semantic Differential
A research technique that employs a seven interval scale rating system for the expression of preference by degrees between a series of polar sets of

measurement. Used to show the respondent's relative commitment to their response choices.

Senior
For marketing purposes, generally considered to be someone age 60 and over. However, programs and services directed to seniors can be found starting as young as age 45. There is no upper limit on senior age, although those 85 years of age and over are sometimes referred to as elderly. The senior market is growing at a faster rate than the rest of the adult market, representing a huge demand for products and services.

Senior Focused Business
A business that allocates a significant portion of its operations to producing and selling goods and services to the senior market, and the extended senior market made up of family, friends, professionals and advisors.

Senior Marketing
Marketing goods and services to people generally over the age of 60. Formally and less commonly known as geriatric marketing.

Sentence Completion Test
A projective technique used in marketing research that employs incomplete sentences to obtain a desired response focus in relation to attitudes and emotions.

Service Mark
Distinctive markings such as symbols and titles used to distinguish goods of one producer from another and registered with Federal or state authorities. Identified by the initials "SM" next to the name, symbol or logo of the service marked object.

Service Quality Variability
Different from products, where quality control can be better managed, service quality may vary considerably from one server to another or even the same server on different days, due to the variability of the human element.

Service User Method
A technique used in survey research to measure service use both before and after exposure to specific promotional messages. The same holds true for product use as well.

Share of Market
The percentage portion of a given market attributable to any of the producers and sellers, in that market, based on dollar volume, number of customers or other units of measure. The given market may be geographic, demographic or both.

Shopper Survey
A survey used on an organization's own contact personnel in an effort to judge their customer service

performance. May also be used to survey competitive operations for comparison. Rewards are sometimes given for superior service by the organization's own staff.

Silent Partner

A partner or investor in a business venture who may not be involved in the day to day operation and is generally unknown to people outside the business relationship.

Simulation Research

A research technique for imitating market conditions and known variables in a programmed model for analysis.

Situation Advertising

An advertising approach that attempts to place the reader in a particular situation as outlined in an advertisement. The goal is to create a buy-in to the message in an effort to generate action.

Situational Analysis

A marketing assessment of the present standing of an organization or program by looking at strengths, weaknesses, opportunities and threats, from both internal and external perspectives. Also commonly referred to as a SWOT analysis.

Slogan

A condensed phrase used in advertising and sales promotion for putting across a main idea or theme. To be recognized and successful, a slogan must be used over and over for an extended period of time.

Social Cause Marketing

The promotion of products, services and programs for social causes directed to a particular group supporting contemporary humanitarian issues.

Soft Goods

Non-durable goods such as clothing and paper goods, as opposed to hard goods.

Soft Sell

A "no pressure" approach to selling with little or no customer prodding after a sales offer has been presented. The focus is put on building a customer relationship first.

Special

A term commonly used to describe a one time sale or sale item offered for a specific time period, reinforced by advertising, marked down tags and other attention grabbers.

Specialty Salespeople

Sales professionals who work only with specific products or product lines and know them in great detail. Typically includes sales of a more technical or complicated nature.

Spec Sheet
A sheet or series of sheets providing the details and specifications of a product or service, especially important for technical or more complex items. While the spec sheets are of value to the salesperson and the presentation, they are also used as supporting material for the prospect.

Spiff
An incentive premium give-away or freebie used as an introduction of a company, product or service or a particular promotion.

Standard Metropolitan Statistical Area (SMSA)
A geographical delineation, determined by the U.S. Census Bureau, designated to areas having a central city with a population of at least 50,000, and sometimes including surrounding counties socially and economically related to the subject city.

Standing Order
An automatically renewable sales order for replenishment based on a pre-arranged agreement. Typically this would continue for the duration of the agreement or until cancelled.

Statement Stuffers
Advertising and promotional messages included in a monthly statement billing, used to generate additional business. May include incentive coupons. An opportunity exists to sell statement stuffer space to non-competing organizations, as well.

Strategic Marketing
The result of a process of developing and maintaining a strategic balance between the organization's marketing goals and its ability to maximize marketing opportunities.

Strategic Plan
The organization's principal marketing and financial plans over a given time frame, supported by the corporate mission. The plan will contain a series of objectives, each supported by specific goals and action plans designed for achieving the objectives.

Stratification
The breaking down of a market or market segment into separate strata for a more definitive analysis and pinpoint marketing.

Subagent
One who is engaged to act on behalf of an agent in the course of his execution of duties for a

principal. Unless prohibited by contract, the hiring of a subagent would be at the discretion of the agent.

Sub goal
See Secondary Goal.

Subhead
A term referring to a short lead-in statement in an advertisement to quickly summarize or reinforce the ad's content.

Success Story
A successful sales event that can be retold in other sales presentations, and used in promotional efforts to make them seem more personalized and timely.

Survey Reliability
The degree to which the results of a given survey can be accepted as valid. Such things as sample size, sample selection, questionnaire design and interviewer training can have a significant role in reliability.

Sweepstakes
A form of sales promotion offering those who enter a contest an opportunity for attractive prizes. Winners may be chosen by random drawing or by a pre-numbered entry form.

Sweetener
An added feature to a sale or contract to make the offer more attractive to the potential customer of that particular offer.

SWOT Analysis
See Situational Analysis.

Systematic Research
Marketing research carried out in a planned, organized and controlled manner, structured according to the desired results.

Systematic Sampling
A method of sample selection where a random starting point is selected and thereafter every nth item is selected to yield the desired sample size.

T

Tabloid
A smaller size newspaper generally having five columns as opposed to a more standard eight columns.

Tag Line
The ending statement or term strategically placed at the closing of a promotional message to emphasize the intent of that message. It may be done in a dramatic or humorous fashion, or as a slogan for emphasis.

Take One Display
A display placard with an advertising tear-off pad, information cards or brochures on counter tops, desks and on transit systems, free for the taking. These are used to strategically target promotional messages.

Tally Sheet
A form used for research data tabulation, allowing for the recording of all responses on one or a set of pages. This arrangement provides for easier data entry, checking or audit.

Target Market
The ideal customer group for the strategic marketing of products, services or programs. Identified through various research techniques, this is the demographic, geographic, and sometimes psychographic, ideal market.

Tariff
A tax or duty due on the shipment or receipt of goods. Tariffs are often used to control the importation of merchandise to protect home produced goods. Tariffs are a necessary consideration in international marketing.

Team Selling
A sales effort that employs two or more sales and support personnel working together to successfully close sales. The group may include technical or professional support.

Telemarketing
A sales by telephone solicitation program based on a goal of so many successes per snumber of contacts. This marketing endeavor has been limited and monitored by Federal, state and local restrictions due to the excesses of some telemarketing firms, sometimes under the guise of research.

Telephone Sales

As opposed to telemarketing where sales calls are made from lists and on spec, telephone sales are typically follow-up calls from previous presentations or incoming calls requesting information and placing orders.

Television Marketing

A growing direct marketing tool through the advancement of cable television, paid programming, infomercials and home shopping channels that provide opportunities for direct response pro-motions and programming.

Territory Management

In marketing terms, strategic plans should address how areas or territories will be covered by the full spectrum of marketing initiatives. In sales, assignment of territories should hold each salesperson responsible for management of their own territory.

Testimonials

Satisfied users or celebrities used to promote products and services in an effort to enhance the credibility of the seller and what is being sold. Similar to endorsements while not requiring an authority figure or expert.

Test Market
A market segment selected for the testing of a new product, service or promotion. The particular delineation can be geographic, demographic, economic or any combination of data necessary for the most viable test.

Test Marketing
Prior to the introduction of a new or improved product or service, a sample market test is advised to prove or fine-tune the proposed offering.

Thematic Apperception Test
A projective technique using pictures or a series of pictures in an effort to have the respondent relate a story behind what they have viewed. The purpose of this procedure is to obtain attitudinal and motivational responses to support other marketing research.

Third Cover
The inside of the back cover of a magazine typically used for advertising placement, and considered a prime location.

Tickler File
A reminder system used for follow up as a "to do" list or for customer and prospect calls. This has been done for many years by means of a card file by dates, or by desk and pocket calendars. Now

many variations have been adapted to computers, lap tops and hand held computer devices.

Time Series
Historical data assembled, recorded and analyzed for specified time intervals. This can be a valuable tool in marketing research and pinpointing marketing opportunities.

Total Customer Value
The sum total of value accumulated from a customer relationship over a given time period. This includes, for example, purchases, cross-selling, referrals and "satisfied customer" statements for promotional use. Requires a good CIF data base.

Total Quality Management (TQM)
Applied to marketing, this represents a commitment to provide a coordinated effort to continually work to improve the quality of products, services and programs offered, and the service support and marketing processes used to promote them.

Total Recall
See Unaided Recall.

Tracking
A process of tabulating the results or pull of an advertisement, sales promotion or other marketing initiative. A valuable tool for identifying trends and providing historical reference.

Trade Acceptance
A bill of exchange or delivery acceptance produced by the seller for the signature of the purchaser upon delivery of ordered goods or supplies.

Trade Advertising
Advertising directed to manufacturers and wholesalers in a given product or service market.

Trade Association
A formal group comprised of members and suppliers in a specific industry for the initial benefit of those associated by virtue of membership programs and services.

Trade Name
A descriptive name for a manufacturer, distributor, retailer or other business designed to distinguish the organization from others in the marketplace. If the name is different from that of the corporation, the trade name may be a dba (doing business as).

Trade Position Discount
Discounts given wholesalers or retailers because of their larger quantity purchases by virtue of negotiated agreements.

Trademark
A registered symbol or name applied to products or services to distinguish them from others, and under the protection of Federal or state registration. A "TM" or ® mark is placed beside the name or symbol each time the name is used.

Trading Area
The geographical area from which an organization draws its customer base. This typically is found in an area surrounding the business or branch location. Also referred to as a marketing area.

Traffic Builder
A promotion or incentive used to increase traffic to a retail store, outlet, bank or shopping center. The goal is to create a willingness to venture in by means of an inducement.

Triad
See Sales Triad.

Trial Purchase
One way to get a customer or prospect to purchase is through a trial test of the product or service.

The trial size or time frame should be limited so that a special purchase can be offered while the trial experience is still fresh.

Trust

In sales, trust is a most important factor in relationship selling. A good relationship cannot be formed without trust, and customers will not buy from someone they do not trust. In a less personal sense, trust in an organization and its products or services is also important to repeat business.

Turnover

Customer turnover is a phenomenon important in any marketing effort. Why customers are lost and where they have gone will likely require marketing research, as these facts need to be known. Natural turnover is commonly called attrition.

U

Ultimate Customer
See End User.

Ultra Vires
An agreement entered into or some other action by an organization in excess of its authority under its corporate charter. See Intra Vires.

Unaided Recall
In survey research, interview responses given purely from memory, with no prompting from the interviewer, are commonly referred to as unaided.

Unconditional Guarantee
A guarantee that merchandise will be fully satisfactory or the customer's money will be refunded. The guarantee and the refund may be provided by either the manufacturer or seller, or shared by them.

Under the Counter
Generally illegal payments for goods or services made in an attempt to avoid taxing authorities or to attract higher payments from a limited and desperate market.

Undifferentiated Marketing

A marketing strategy that does not call for segmenting the market, but rather chooses to blanket a whole market with a particular offer. Used more often for goods and services that are less demographically specific.

Undocumented

Events and developments that have not been recorded or documented in literature or available for review. Research findings that are incomplete or unrecorded may be considered undocumented.

Undue Influence

Excessive pressure applied to an individual or corporation in an effort to obtain a desired result. In extreme cases, may involve the use of duress. Excessive sales pressure may result in undue influence and likely a lost sale.

Unfair Competition

A dishonest and usually illegal competitive business practice of taking advantage of others in a given market by means of false claims, misleading advertising, interfering with competitors' operations or marketing efforts, and other means of deception.

Unique Selling Proposition
A marketing strategy designed to strategically position an organization, product or service in a defined target market relative to the competition, thereby achieving a competitive advantage.

Universe
In marketing research, a universe represents the total number of people in a given area or market from which a survey sample is drawn.

Unrestricted Sampling
A random selection of sample units drawn from a total population or universe to be surveyed for research purposes.

Unstructured Questions
Survey questions that are not standardized, permitting interviewer flexibility. These types of questions are chosen for more in depth questioning by more experienced survey takers.

Untapped Market
Potential demand that is not presently being met in a given market area. In this situation an existing, new or improved product or service may solve a current need.

Upscale
A higher priced or premium product, service or market. This term is often applied to newer issues intended to convey a more modern, somewhat pricey image.

U.S. Census Bureau
This government agency is a part of the U.S. Department of Commerce, and provides U.S. census data available to the public. Data are compiled and projected from ten year census collections, published and offered on-line. *The Statistical Abstract of the United States,* published annually, is a good source for this data.

User-Friendly
A product or service designed with the user and the user's needs in mind, less technically complex and relatively easy to use.

User Influence
Often early adaptors, users influence prospective buyers of products and services by their favorable reactions and recommendations. This happens within organizations as well as with family members, close friends and associates.

Usury
A rate of interest charged on a loan that is higher than what is allowed under the law. Such rates are

not typically seen in legal commercial transactions, but more likely to be found in private business relationships.

V

Validity

A measurement of the accuracy of a statistical analysis in a research application. Typically used in connection with survey samples. See Confidence Level.

Value

A quality of a product or service considered highly important to customers. To some, value may be seen as more important than price alone, but the better strategy is to sell on both.

Value Added Reseller

An individual or organization that purchases products or equipment, refurbishes or makes improvements in them, and then resells them as fully working goods.

Value Analysis

A means of determining where cost reductions may be made in a product, service, program or marketing approach and produced less expensively, without sacrificing value. The prescribed approach is to break the item of focus down into its component parts for better analysis.

Value Marketing

A marketing strategy that chooses to focus on the value of the product or service itself and its support services in designing a promotional approach.

Variable

One of a variety of potential characteristics in a marketing research initiative that can have an impact on the outcome of that application. The impact may represent a positive or negative consideration that needs to be identified.

Variance

A difference or deviation to a value or distribution applied in accounting, finance or statistics. In zoning terms, a variance applies to an ordinance or regulation requiring approval.

Vendor

A provider of goods or services to individuals and corporations. Vendors can represent a marketing opportunity in terms of a referral source for new business. They represent a potential information source since they may also serve your competitors.

Venture Capitalist

A person or organization that provides financing for new or expanding ventures. Often, venture capitalists will take on an investment role in exchange for more favorable financing terms.

Verification of Findings
The process of substantiating results developed through research analysis by comparison with known factors, previous research and other historical data.

Vertical Integration
Process by which a manufacturer exercises control over products from raw materials and refinement through delivery to the customer. Advancements in technology, trade legislation and foreign competition have made this a rarer occurrence today.

Vested Interest
An interest in an agreement or property that is fixed by pre-determined terms for present or future rights. Generally, vested interest accrues over time.

Visionary
One who has the ability to look into the future and forecast or project a need or opportunity before others are likely to do so. This is a valuable asset to marketing and strategic planning.

Voice Mail

Commonly used by businesses and individuals, and justified in the name of time and money. However, the use of voice mail is not universally accepted by the public (customers and prospects). While this may be more of an issue in the senior market, it is not unique to that market. Further, it limits customer contact upon which relationships are built.

Voluntary Chain

An independent merchant organization formed for the purpose of purchasing merchandise in larger quantities for greater discounts. This is a means to keeping their prices competitive in the marketplace.

W

Waiting Time
Often seen as time wasted, both customer and seller disdain waiting for one another. Through better planning and familiarity, this can be controlled, but the importance of the first impression must be considered.

Wait-Time Aggravation Index
Due to the importance of lost waiting time to both the vendor and the customer, some organizations have studied the issue to determine what is a realistic "waiting to be served" time frame. Some have devised ways to communicate the estimated wait time to the customer in an effort to keep them happy.

Want
In marketing goods and services, it is important to distinguish the difference between want and need. While a need is an essential, a want is a desired or strived for personal quality of life issue.

Warehouse Clubs
Typically "membership only" lower price retail outlets selling goods to individuals and organizations.

Often goods are offered in larger quantities and emphasize lower per unit prices.

Warranty

A structured guarantee on a product or service for a specific time period and according to certain stated conditions. Warranty particulars are often enclosed in product packaging and require a return acknowledgement.

Wear and Tear

Common physical deterioration in products and other properties as a result of age, use and exposure to the elements. A condition not usually covered by warranty.

Wear-out Factor

One of a number of variables that may create a condition causing the effectiveness of repeated advertising or promotion to decline to the point of being ineffective.

Wear Out Mailing

The use of direct mail for select advertising materials to the same market area until a profitable number of responses can no longer be achieved.

Webmaster

A designated staff member or hired professional who is responsible for the maintenance of a web site on the World Wide Web (www).

What If Analysis

Similar to a sensitivity or SWOT Analysis, this is an attempt to gauge the consequences of acting or not acting on a condition or opportunity in the marketplace.

White Space

The unused space surrounding an advertisement or other message in print media. Some advertisers use more or less white space for the emphasis or design they desire.

Wholesale Club

See Warehouse Clubs.

Wholesaler

A producer or distributor offering larger quantities of goods who sells or resells them to retailers and other merchants.

Widget

The proverbial hypothetical name for a given item of production used as an example in business case studies. May also be used to refer to an unnamed item for the sake of calling it something until further identified.

Window of Opportunity
A timeframe within which a prime opportunity may exist in a given market for the introduction of a product, service, program or promotional campaign.

Win-Win Strategy
The most successful sales strategies in personal selling are ones where there is an apparent net gain for both buyer and seller. To be successful, the salesperson needs to convey this equation to the customer.

Word Association Test
A projective research technique for drawing out image and attitude responses through the use of various cue words. The researcher will provide specific cues either verbally or by handing the respondent a list to read from and choose a response.

Word of Mouth Advertising
Generally, an informal spreading of favorable communication about a product, service or program from satisfied customers to prospective customers. While difficult to harness as a formal

means of advertising, it is an effective business generator.

Working Capital
A financial arrangement from a lender, providing time for a producer to get goods and services to market which can provide the necessary cash flow to pay back the lender.

Work in Process
A project or task presently in a state of being developed or completed, but not ready for presentation. May apply to any stage in a process prior to completion.

Work in Progress
A project or event that is presently underway, as yet incomplete, but progressing according to a specific plan and timetable.

X, Y, Z

Xtra

An advertising language substitute for the word Extra, used for effect and to gain attention, particularly in newspapers.

Yellow Pages

A bound directory, typically published in conjunction with the telephone directory. Businesses have found through tabulation that a defined segment of their customer base shops by means of the Yellow Pages.

Yes or No Response

A research questionnaire technique whereby the respondent is forced to choose one of two bipolar responses. This provides for no subjectivity on the part of either the respondent or the researcher.

Yield

In research terms, refers to the results of a survey sample response. In a promotional effort, yield refers to direct responses, often in the form of coupons or response cards. In finance, yield represents a return on investment.

Zero Base Budgeting
A budgeting method that requires justification for all items, new or repeat, in the annual budgeting process, based on relative merit.

Zone Pricing
Pricing by defined geographic areas or zones, based on the cost of providing goods and services to specific areas versus other areas, for shipping and handling costs.

About the Author

Michael C. Walker recently retired from active management after serving as Chief Executive of Seniorsfirst (Presbyterian Homes and Services of Genesee Valley, Inc.) and its predecessors for twenty-four years. Seniorsfirst is a full service provider of facilities, services and programs to the senior market in the greater Rochester, New York area. These include independent living, assisted living, home delivered services, adult day programs, home healthcare, nursing home care, including transitional and rehabilitative care, among others.

Mr. Walker was responsible for the design and implementation of an innovative program serving seniors in their own homes. The award-winning Club 24 Senior Living At Home® program has been replicated across the United States using this unique model.

Prior to his most recent employment, Mr. Walker served 15 years for the predecessors of J.P. Morgan Chase Manhattan Bank in upstate New York as a Vice President in marketing and finance. During his banking career he wrote *An Introduction to Bank Marketing Research*, published by the Bank Marketing Association, Chicago, the first book of its kind in the banking industry. The book was later reprinted in Europe and translated into Spanish.

While Mr. Walker has retired from active management, he has not retired from working. He continues to be actively engaged as a marketing and management consultant to organizations and businesses in the senior market.

He is also the author of two recently published marketing books now available through 1st Books Library. *Marketing to Seniors* unveils a number of unique aspects of the senior market, including the introduction of the "extended senior customer" to account for the involvement of others in senior purchasing decisions. These include family, friends, advisors and healthcare professionals. *Home Delivered Services: Building and Maintaining Your Program* provides a "how to" approach to the replication of a home services program much like Club 24 Senior Living at Home®, including how to successfully market it profitably. These books may be ordered through the publisher at www.1stBooks.com, (800/839-8640), or through your local bookstore.